BFI TV Classics

BFI TV Classics is a series of books celebrating key individual television programmes and series. Television scholars, critics and novelists provide critical readings underpinned with careful research, alongside a personal response to the programme and a case for its 'classic' status.

Also Published:

Doctor Who
Kim Newman

The Office
Ben Walters

Our Friends in the North
Michael Eaton

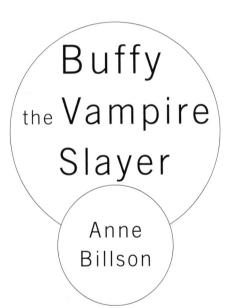

Buffy
the Vampire
Slayer

Anne
Billson

 Publishing

First published in 2005 by the
British Film Institute
21 Stephen Street, London W1T 1LN

Editor: Rob White

The British Film Institute's purpose is to champion moving image culture in all its richness and diversity across the UK, for the benefit of as wide an audience as possible, and to create and encourage debate.

Images from *Buffy the Vampire Slayer* © Twentieth Century-Fox Film Corporation. Page 5 – *Thunderbirds*, ITC Entertainment/Apf TV for ATV; page 7 – *The Avengers* © Canal +; page 8 – *X-Men/Kitty Pryde* © Marvel Entertainment Group; page 10 – *Modesty Blaise* © Modesty Blaise Ltd; page 11 – *Come Drink with Me*, Shaw Brothers; page 13 – *Coffy*, American International Productions; page 14 – *Noroît*, Sunchild Productions; page 15 – *Aliens* © Twentieth Century-Fox Film Corporation; page 23 – *Buffy the Vampire Slayer* (the movie), Sandollar Productions/Kuzui Enterprises/ Twentieth Century-Fox Film Corporation; page 137 – *Fray* © Joss Whedon/Dark Horse Comics.

Whilst considerable effort has been made to correctly identify the copyright holders, this has not been possible in all cases. We apologise for any omissions or mistakes in the credits and we will endeavour to remedy, in future editions, errors brought to our attention by the relevant rights holder.

None of the content of this publication is intended to imply that it is endorsed by the programme's broadcaster or production companies involved.

British Library Cataloguing-in-Publication Data
A catalogue record for this book is available from the British Library

ISBN 1–84457–089–4

Set by Fakenham Photosetting Ltd, Fakenham, Norfolk
Printed in the UK by Butler and Tanner Limited, Frome, Somerset

Contents

Acknowledgments

Special thanks to Philippe Aulié, Angie Errigo, Kim Newman, Lucretia Stewart. Extra-special thanks to Rob White.

1 Before *Buffy*

I'm a telly baby. I was born into the postwar generation that grew up
with television. This brave new medium would become our sibling and
playmate, nursemaid and teacher. The programmes we watched so
avidly in our childhood would one day take their place in our dating and
mating rituals – hazy pre-video memories of *Bill and Ben* or *Whirligig*,
F Troop or *Doctor Who* exchanged in a quest for common ground. My
first experience of the generation gap was when I started meeting people
who couldn't remember *Prudence Kitten*, or *Boots and Saddles*, or the
newsflash announcing that President Kennedy had been shot.

I watched a huge amount of television back then, as did
everyone I knew, with the exception of one classmate whose Luddite
parents had banned it from their home. With a choice of only two
channels, we would all watch the same programmes and discuss them
at school the next day, but although I tried to share my friends'
enthusiasm for *Coronation Street* (1960–) or *Emergency – Ward 10*
(1957–67), soap operas never seized my imagination the way that
Westerns or *The Man from U.N.C.L.E.* (1964–8) did. Nobody thought
it odd that I preferred heroic action to domestic drama; they assumed it
was because I fancied the male stars – David McCallum, say, or James
Drury. But if I identified with anyone, it was with the Cowboys and
Indians rather than the women who cowered in the middle of the
wagon circle while the menfolk did all the fighting. I mentally shifted
genders as a matter of course, without even being aware that I was
having to make the adjustment. Many years later, I read about a piece

of graffiti, spotted in a women's lavatory in New York, that seemed to sum up a lifetime's experience of watching action stories written and shot from a male point of view: 'When you watch the film *Vertigo*, are you Scottie wanting Madeleine, or are you Madeleine wanting Scotty to want you? Or both alternatively and simultaneously?'[1] I was all those things, and more.

It wasn't until I was watching the final episode of the final season of *Buffy the Vampire Slayer* that a long-buried memory stirred at the back of my brain. In this episode, Buffy's friend Willow casts a spell enabling Buffy to share her hitherto exclusive superpowers with vast numbers of adolescent girls, who suddenly find themselves possessed of the strength and skill to fight back against the legions of vampires pouring out of hell. Shazzam! These girls were all action heroines! And, at that point, I remembered that when I was ten years old, maybe even younger, I too used to think of myself as an 'action heroine', though I would never have used those words back then. In my secret fantasies, I would rescue the most popular girls in my class from evildoers who would have locked them in remote towers or chained them to dungeon walls for reasons that my innocent prepubescent self couldn't begin to comprehend. Even though in real life I was rubbish at sports, the rescue would invariably involve acrobatic feats, swordfights and scaling castle walls, and the popular girls, once rescued, would be humbled and grateful, as well as surprised and intrigued that this quiet classmate to whom they'd never paid much attention was not as uninteresting as she appeared. That she was, in fact, a superheroine who had been leading an exciting and glamorous double life.

This was thirty years before the heroines of *Buffy the Vampire Slayer* or *Alias* (2001–) or *Xena: Warrior Princess* (1995–2002) kicked all manner of evil ass on a weekly basis. The young girls of today don't know how lucky they are; thanks to Buffy, they're spoilt for choice. It's clear to me now, thinking back, that I was continually if unconsciously searching for female role models in the popular culture of my childhood. The problem was that there weren't any, at least not in the TV shows and films and books I knew. Girls were annoying, like Violet Elizabeth in Richmal Crompton's *Just William* books, or insipid, like the schoolgirls of Enid Blyton's school stories. Or, like Snow White or the Sleeping Beauty, they were victims, forced to rely on handsome princes to get them out of trouble. I suppose it was symptomatic that, when it came to fairy tales, I was always more impressed by the witches, especially since in the Disney cartoon versions, they were not just powerful but glamorous – at least before they morphed into dragons or crones. I grew up fascinated by evil women, from the Wicked Witch of the West from *The Wizard of Oz* (1939), to Cruella De Vil from *101 Dalmatians* (1960), to Milady de Winter in the BBC's 1966 serialisation of *The Three Musketeers*. Milady had a fleur-de-lys branded into her shoulder, kept a poisoned dagger by the bed and repeatedly stood up to the manly musketeers, who were able to cut her down to size only by summoning the Executioner of Lille to chop off her head on what I considered the flimsiest of pretexts. I was outraged when a well-meaning aunt gave me a children's edition of the Alexandre Dumas novel in which all traces of Milady had been excised, leaving nothing but a story about men fighting men. And where's the fun in that?

3

I was drawn to these women not because they were evil, but because they were anything but simpering victims. They played second fiddle to no man; they had their own agenda, and if that involved unleashing flying monkey demons or kidnapping spotty dogs or poisoning a duplicitous lover's mistress – well, at least their lives were more exciting than those of the other female characters glimpsed on television, in films or in advertising; women so bland they barely registered on my childhood radar. I couldn't understand why Samantha from *Bewitched* (1964–72) had opted for the life of a housewife, married to a drab mortal (Darwen, was it? Or Durwood?), forced to keep her spell-casting under wraps instead of indolently wafting around in chiffon gowns like her mother, Endora. I sometimes wonder whether my continuing fascination with the horror genre – which has endured long past the age when we're supposed to have grown out of such foolery – had its roots in those early days, when the only decent female role models I could find were those who dabbled in black magic and murder.

Back in the 1950s and 1960s, action heroes were exclusively male. The stories in girls' comics were lacking in life-or-death situations, so I gravitated towards my older brother's weeklies, which were packed with more colourful yarns about invading aliens or man-eating dinosaurs. My favourite TV programme was *The Lone Ranger* (1949–57) and my favourite character was Tonto. There were two things I wanted to be when I grew up: a ballerina and a Red Indian, preferably both at once. But I had no intention of being a squaw, confined to the wigwam, tending papooses or rustling up buffalo stew; I wanted to be a brave with long hair, feathers and weapons. On the other hand, I wasn't interested in being a tomboy in short hair and trousers, like George in Enid Blyton's *Famous Five* stories. My heroic ideal, I realise now, was something that simply didn't exist when I was growing up: a beautiful heroine with long hair and pretty clothes – a heroine who *looked* like a princess, but who nevertheless battled cowboys, musketeers and man-eating dinosaurs.

Vampires had yet to enter the equation. It would be years before I would pass as old enough to sneak into X-rated movies, and my first glimpse of a vampire, on an early episode of *Doctor Who*, might have been quickly forgotten had not my older brother afterwards taken a sadistic delight in lurking in dark corners and intoning, 'I am Count Dracula', in a heavy foreign accent. I was sufficiently intrigued to start scouring film magazines for pictures of the Count and his cohorts. I became a vampire expert in embryo. (One of the biggest disappointments of my childhood was the discovery that the TV series *Batman* (1966–8), starring Adam West, had absolutely nothing to do with vampires, or even bats.) I was familiar with the faces of Christopher Lee and Peter Cushing long before I'd watched them in any of their starring roles, though the title that excited me the most was that of a 1963 Hammer film called *Kiss of the Vampire*. Even back then, the idea of kissing, or being kissed by, one of these horrible yet fascinating creatures gave me a guilty thrill.

Imagine how excited I would have been if I had been able to watch a TV show combining the beautiful long-haired heroine of my dreams with pretty clothes, swordfights, kissing *and* vampires.

It was children's television that eventually provided me with my first female role model. She was a puppet on *Thunderbirds* (1965–6). The Tracy brothers were interchangeable (apart from Deep Space John, whom I quite fancied), but Lady Penelope was a class act, more than just a gussied-up Woodentop. She was blonde, chic and independently wealthy: a cross between Jackie Kennedy and Lady Antonia Fraser, with added strings. She knew how to handle a gun and kept a cool head even when tied up in the path of an oncoming express train. She answered to no man; men answered to her, notably her chauffeur, Parker, who drove her around in a pink Rolls Royce. She spoke in a sort of cultivated murmur. And she was the proud possessor of the ultimate girly gadget – a powder compact cum two-way radio. I was so smitten that I bought the Lady Penelope comic and wore the free Lady Penelope X-Ray specs and practised the Lady Penelope walk – a sort of jerky wooden skip – on

5

The first TV action heroine? Lady Penelope takes it easy in *Thunderbirds*

my way home from school. As an action heroine she had her limits; unlike the puppets in *Team America* (2004) twenty years later, she didn't do kung-fu, but at the age of eleven I'd never even heard of martial arts so I didn't miss it.

Fortunately, my next and most important pre-Buffy female role model turned out to be a heroine of flesh and blood, albeit one who existed in a fantasy world. Unlike Lady Penelope, Emma Peel of *The Avengers* (1961–9) *did* practise a rudimentary form of karate. She was the successor to Cathy Gale (before my time) and never subservient to John Steed, her partner-in-adventure. Though she was married, she was the very opposite of the *Bewitched*-style housewife; we never saw her husband, and neither, apparently, did she. The 'Mrs' tag was a cunning ploy to grant her autonomy, enabling her to flirt with Steed but imposing limits so the flirtation was never in danger of tipping over into anything mushy, which would have relegated her to mere love interest. Mrs Peel's habitual facial expression was an ironic smile, often accompanied by a quizzically arched eyebrow. She was sophisticated, witty and though, in her first season, she was continually being captured and tied up and rescued by Steed, she never panicked or acted helpless. She wasn't a decorative appendage, she was his equal – unlike female sidekicks in shows such as *Doctor Who* or *Adam Adamant Lives!* (1966–7), whose function seemed to be to provide an irritating counterpoint of hysteria or stupidity to the cool-headed male heroes. When, thirty years later, I encountered Diana Rigg in a queue for the ladies' lavatories at the Savoy, I couldn't help blurting out, 'You were my role model!' She replied, very graciously I thought in the circumstances, 'Why thank you,' before I remembered my manners and added, 'And you still are.'

Mrs Peel proved that heroines could be feminine and feisty at the same time. She also proved they could be sexy without being reduced to a dumb sex object. In 'A Touch of Brimstone', she dresses as the Queen of Sin in a costume only a whisker away from full-blown S&M gear: tight boots, spiked collar, figure-hugging black corset. She looks like a male adolescent's wet dream, obviously, but this doesn't stop her

7

Emma Peel in *The Avengers*: 'You were my role model!'

from frowning disapprovingly at the villain's description of women as 'mere vessels of pleasure'. It's no exaggeration to say that watching *The Avengers* in the Mrs Peel era was the highlight of my life. My diaries for these years are full of entries such as: 'Had bath and washed hair. Watched Avengers and now feel glam,' or 'Did loads of prep. Washed hair and had bath and watched Avengers. Feel Avengerish.' (Evidently the life of the average 1960s teenager was not so thrill-packed with sex and drugs and rock 'n' roll as we are nowadays led to believe.) Mrs Peel was my kind of woman. I was so besotted with her, that when in 1968 she quit the series (that MIA husband had finally turned up) and was replaced by the dizzy Tara King, who was neither as pretty (cropped hair, for heaven's sake!) nor as clever, nor as skilled at fighting, a light went out of my life and I stopped watching.

Had I but known it, female action heroes were already beginning to infiltrate Marvel and DC superhero comics in the 1960s. Since these were strictly the province of boys and hard to come by in

Teenage superheroine: Kitty Pryde of *X-Men*

those parts of Croydon where I grew up, they passed me by, though I did get my hands on a few copies of *The Fantastic Four*, featuring Sue Storm alias Invisible Girl, though I reckoned being invisible was less exciting than, say, turning into a human torch. All unseen by me, Super Girl and Bat Girl were mere afterthoughts to their better known sires, but Wonder Woman ('beautiful as Aphrodite, wise as Athena, stronger than Hercules and swifter than Mercury') had made her debut back in 1941 and Jean Grey alias Marvel Girl (and later Phoenix) was already making her bow in the original line-up of *X-Men*. In the 1970s, she would be joined by Ororo Munroe alias Storm and, in the 1980s, by Kitty Pryde alias Shadowcat, a teenage girl with the power to pass through solid matter. Joss Whedon, creator of *Buffy the Vampire Slayer*, has acknowledged Kitty as one of the inspirations for Buffy. But teenage superheroines were a long time coming, and more often than not they were part of a team rather than individuals in ther own right. One of the best things about Buffy is that, ultimately, she got to be both at once – part of a team *and* an independent operator.

The one comic-strip heroine I did stumble across was Peter O'Donnell's *Modesty Blaise*, who started life as a cartoon strip in 1963 in the London *Evening Standard*, though I first discovered her in a series of novels (again by O'Donnell) published a few years later. Here, at last, was a worthy female counterpart to James Bond – a beautiful secret agent with a mysterious past, innumerable male admirers and a sprinkling of what was, for a pubescent girl in the 1960s, exciting amounts of nudity and sex. I was probably the only twelve-year-old in the world who rushed out to see Joseph Losey's 1966 film version, starring Monica Vitti. I confidently looked forward to seeing more kick-ass heroines like Emma and Modesty.

Except there weren't any. It was as though Emma Peel had never existed, and in the 1970s television ceased to be of vital importance to my life; at long last, I had better things to do than wash my hair and feel Avengerish. I was vaguely aware of *Police Woman* (1974–8), though Sgt Pepper Anderson seemed to spend more time disguised as a gangster's moll in fishnet stockings than engaged in active police work.

10

Secret agent woman: *Modesty Blaise*

Charlie's Angels (1976–81) was an insult to my nascent feminist sensibility (which unfortunately went hand-in-hand with a temporary sense of humour bypass, though compared to the twenty-first-century film versions, the original TV series now looks almost politically correct), while *Wonder Woman* (1976–9) was just too camp to take seriously. The 1980s weren't much better, though Alexis in *Dynasty* (1981–9) was a soap-opera variation on Servalan, Supreme Bitch of the Universe on *Blake's 7* (1978–81), while *Cagney and Lacey* (1982–8) gave TV cop shows their first strong, realistic female characters, whose emotional lives were given as much weight as the cases they had to deal with. For my taste, though, they were a little too drab. In any case, in the 1970s and 1980s, instead of sitting at home watching television, I was going to the cinema.

11

The martial arts heroine of *Come Drink with Me*

Hollywood in the 1970s turned out some of the most subversive, original and provocative movies ever made, but great roles for women were distinguished chiefly by their absence. Typically, foreign films and exploitation movies stepped in where the Hollywood mainstream couldn't be bothered to tread, but it wasn't until the mid-1970s that these alternative action heroines began to trickle into British repertory cinemas or on to late-night bills. Gravity-defying kung-fu artistes such as Pei-Pei Cheng in *Lady Hermit* (1968) and *Come Drink with Me* (1969), Feng Hsu in *A Touch of Zen* (1969) and half the cast of *The Fate of Lee Khan* (1973) paved the way for the female action stars in *Crouching Tiger, Hidden Dragon* (2000) and *House of Flying Daggers* (2004) three decades later, and made dear Emma Peel's karate chops look ever-so-English and genteel. Angela Mao, one of the actresses in *The Fate of Lee Khan*, gained something of a reputation as a female Bruce Lee thanks to starring roles in *Hapkido* (1970) and *When Taekwondo Strikes* (1973), though in *Enter the Dragon* (1973), the first American-produced kung-fu film and therefore the first kung-fu movie I ever saw, she was relegated to a supporting role as Bruce's sister, doomed to die and thus provide him with a personal motive to kick the villain's ass. But many of the women in Chinese action films were more than mere sidekicks or girlfriends or sisters; they were heroines with a purpose, using their martial-arts skills to combat evil.

Meanwhile, on the Blaxploitation front, Tamara Dobson cracked down on drug trafficking in *Cleopatra Jones* (1973), while in *Coffy* (1973) Pam Grier posed as a hooker, concealing weapons in her Afro, to wreak vengeance on the dealers responsible for the drug-addled state of her eleven-year-old sister. Grier posed as a hooker again in *Foxy Brown* (1974) to wreak yet more vengeance on drug dealers, this time the ones who killed her boyfriend. The plots of Blaxploitation films, like kung-fu movies, were generally propelled by revenge, a motive that was to figure in *Buffy the Vampire Slayer* only rarely, and even then depicted as negative and destructive, but the TV series pays homage to Buffy's Blaxploitation forebears in flashbacks to 1970s New York City featuring an Afro-coiffed vampire slayer called Nikki.

The Blaxploitation heroine in action in *Coffy*

Even European art-house films produced spunkier women than the average Hollywood blockbuster. The semi-improvisational fantasies of Jacques Rivette were spun around female characters who dabbled in magic, like the heroines of *Céline et Julie vont en bateau* (1974), or the beautiful witches of *Duelle* (1976) who fought each other on the streets of Paris for possession of a mysterious jewel, or the female pirates of *Noroît* (1976), in which the women cross swords on the decks of galleons or in crumbling castles while token men look on from the sidelines.

It wasn't until 1979 that the first bona fide Hollywood action heroine made her bow. It's symptomatic that she burst on to the screen in a then-despised fantasy genre, a B-movie plot given classy A-movie treatment.

Nikki the Vampire Slayer: homage to Blaxploitation

The Pirate Queen (left) in Jacques Rivette's *Noroît*

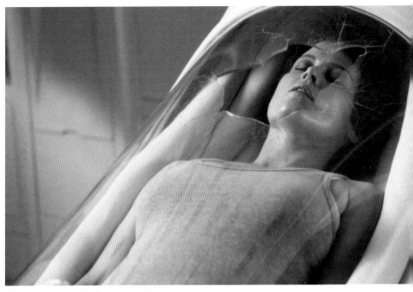

Ripley: the first Hollywood Action Heroine

Alien, an old-dark-house horror movie transposed to outer space, turned gender stereotyping upside-down with a female character who went about her business in a no-nonsense manner, and who tackled the monster without screaming or tripping over her high heels or getting hysterical about broken fingernails. Not only that, but she ended up the sole human survivor while her male colleagues (and one hysterical female) all perished. In the original screenplay, the character of Ripley was male, but by casting the imposing Sigourney Weaver in the role, the film-makers proved that anything a guy could do, a girl could do just as well. And by the time the film came out, I'd got over my adolescent obsession with pretty clothes, so Ripley's grimy overalls didn't put me off too much.

With each sequel – *Aliens* (1986), *Alien³* (1992) and *Alien: Resurrection* (1997, screenplay by Joss Whedon), the character of Ripley developed in new and unexpected ways: surrogate mother, sci-fi Joan of Arc, alien–human hybrid, but always female and always kick-ass, with an agenda that didn't involve staying at home with the papooses and cooking buffalo stew, but big subjects such as life and death, good and evil, survival, death and resurrection and blasting monsters to kingdom come – much like the subjects Buffy would tackle a couple of decades later, in between kissing her vampire boyfriends and shopping for clothes.

Despite the box-office success of the first two *Alien* films, Hollywood in the 1980s wasn't exactly overrun by female action heroes. Ripley was a one-off. Her nearest rival was Sarah Connor in *The Terminator* (1984) who starts out as an airheaded waitress but undergoes intensive gender-role re-education while being chased by an unstoppable killer robot and emerges a tough self-sufficient heroine, albeit a pregnant one whose chief function in the plot is to be mother to the man who will lead mankind's struggle against the machines. In the first sequel, *Terminator 2: Judgment Day* (1991), Connor is even tougher, with biceps, guerrilla training and a roll-up dangling from her lips. But she's still the hero's mum, rather than a heroine in her own right. Otherwise, in terms of strong female role models, the 1980s carried on where the 1970s had left off. In film after film, Hollywood women were decorative afterthoughts to the main event, their function to provide the hero with romantic or sexual relief, or be placed in jeopardy so they could be rescued, or simply to titillate male audiences with a display of flesh.

This, then, was the state of play in 1992, when a high-school horror comedy came along and introduced not just a new kind of heroine, but the kind of heroine for whom I'd been searching all my life. By then I was so cynical and jaded that I didn't recognise her straight away. How ironic that her creator was a man.

2 The Chosen One

Joss Whedon, born in 1964, is a third-generation TV writer. His grandfather, John Whedon, wrote for *The Dick Van Dyke Show* (1961–6), *The Andy Griffith Show* (1960–8) and *Leave It to Beaver* (1957–63). His father, Tom Whedon, wrote for *The Golden Girls* (1985–92). Sitcoms run in the family. Whedon earned his writing spurs on episodes of *Roseanne* (1988–97) and *Parenthood* (1990–1), a short-lived series based on the 1989 movie of the same name. He worked as uncredited script doctor on *Speed* (1994), *Waterworld* (1995) and *Twister* (1996) and was credited with the screenplays of *Toy Story* (1995), *Alien: Resurrection* and *Titan AE* (2000). But the first of his original screenplays to go into production was *Buffy the Vampire Slayer*.

 Buffy the Vampire Slayer wasn't the first film to fuse horror and teen movies. The first time I encountered the word 'prom' was the tagline, 'If you've got a taste for terror, take Carrie to the prom'. But the blood-splattered climax at the school dance in *Carrie* (1976), adapted from the Stephen King novel, was preceded by almost voyeuristic scenes of high-school life with its cliques, cruelty and adolescent rites of passage that for socially inadequate outsiders are nothing short of hell. Unlike Buffy, poor Carrie White doesn't have a back-up team of supportive friends and relatives, with the result that her telekinetic superpowers run riot. Two years later, the success of the low-budget *Halloween* (1978), with its high-school students stalked and slaughtered by a masked psychopath, unleashed a new wave of slasher movies aimed at teenage audiences: *Friday the 13th* (1980) and sequels, as well as *Prom Night* (1980), *Terror Train* (1981), *The Burning* (1981), *Hell Night* (1981), *My Bloody Valentine* (1981), *Rosemary's Killer* (1981) and so on. Standing out from the crowd was *A Nightmare on Elm Street* (1984), which, although its sequels degenerated into parades of special effects capped by callous one-liners, was an ingenious riff on the slasher subgenre; this time the line between fantasy and reality became interestingly blurred as the psychopath stalked the teenagers in their dreams. *Buffy the Vampire Slayer*, film and series, would make repeated use of dream sequences, and would simultaneously embrace and subvert the clichés of slasher movies in a postmodern approach even more radical than that of *Scream* (1996) and its sequels (lampooned in their turn by *Scary Movie* [2000] and its sequels).

But although Laurie in *Halloween* and Nancy in *A Nightmare on Elm Street* are courageous, resourceful heroines who fight back against the bogeymen and survive (to become examples of what Carol J. Clover refers to in her book *Men, Women and Chainsaws: Gender in the Modern Horror Film* as 'The Final Girl'),[2] by and large the girls in slasher movies do little but get their kit off, take showers, scream, flee and die. In the 1980s, women in real life had come a long way, it seemed to me, but the women in horror films were the same old stupid victims.

By the 1990s, vampires were no longer the mysterious X-rated creatures that had fascinated me as a child. Vampire movies had changed. In the 1970s, film-makers tried to spice up the bloodsucking formula by adding extra ingredients (much as Spike the vampire would later spice up his daily helping of blood by adding crumbled Weetabix). The most popular added ingredient, of course, was sex, which at least resulted in more female characters, even if they tended to be vampires with softcore lesbian tendencies in films like *The Vampire Lovers* (1970) and *Lust for a Vampire* (1971). But there was a significant amount of interbreeding between other genres as well, such as *Captain Kronos, Vampire Hunter* (1973), a low-budget vampire comedy-action-adventure featuring an enigmatic, dope-smoking, sword-wielding hero, written and directed by

Brian Clemens, author of many classic episodes of *The Avengers*. Alas, the movie was a flop, scuppering plans for a franchise, and the shifting of emphasis from vampires to the people who hunted them was put on hold until Buffy came along. Hammer's last vampire movie was a collaboration with Hong Kong's Shaw Brothers, a vampire–kung fu hybrid called *The Legend of the Seven Golden Vampires* (1974), which didn't really cut the mustard on either a vampire or a kung-fu level, though it did have its moments, mostly involving semi-naked sacrificial maidens, and anticipated Buffy's fighting style – a combination of karate, kick-boxing, gymnastics and fisticuffs. Let's call it Buffy-fu.

    With the exception of *Dracula AD 1972* (1972), Hammer's vampires were rooted firmly in the past, in Bram Stoker's Victorian England or a Bray Studios version of nineteenth-century Mittel Europe. But Stephen King's novel *Salem's Lot* (1975) dragged the myth out of the gothic crypt and into smalltown America, while George Romero's film *Martin* (1976) updated it to industrial Pennsylvania, where a confused modern teenager compensates for his lack of fangs with syringes and razor blades. One might wonder why vampires, with their traditional aversion to sunlight, would seek out sunnier climes, but Dracula had already relocated to contemporary Southern California as early as 1958 (*The Return of Dracula*), and in the 1970s he was joined there by *Count Yorga* (1970) who found plenty of snack food in modern Los Angeles. The telefilm, *The Night Stalker* (1971), features a wisecracking reporter versus a vampire on the streets of modern Las Vegas, and, in a mildly feminist twist, *The Velvet Vampire* (1971) begins with a female vampire turning the tables on a would-be rapist on the mean streets of Los Angeles. The female characters in these films were vampires or victims, however, never the hunters. Phallic staking rituals were always the province of the menfolk.

    Although Bud and Lou met Dracula in *Abbott and Costello Meet Frankenstein* (1948) and horror and comedy merged to haunting effect in Roman Polanksi's *Dance of the Vampires* (1968), it wasn't until the end of the 1970s that bloodsucking was played for laughs in films such as *Love at First Bite* (1979) in which Dracula falls in love with a

19

New York model, or *Once Bitten* (1985), in which Lauren Hutton sinks her fangs into a young Jim Carrey, as well as a clutch of other low-budget films with such self-explanatory titles as *My Best Friend Is a Vampire* (1988), *Beverly Hills Vamp* (1988) and *Teen Vamp* (1988). *Vamp* (1986) was a non-comic spin on the same formula, pitting young male college students against a fanged Grace Jones and vampire strippers.

     More interesting, for me, was *Fright Night* (1985), a variation on the Boy Who Cried Wolf, about a teenage boy who suspects his neighbour is a vampire – as indeed he is! He's certainly more alluring than the bland young hero, though the presence of a devoted male human minder suggests this is a vampire who might swing both ways. There was even more of a homoerotic vibe in *The Lost Boys* (1987), in which fanged juvenile delinquents terrorise a small Californian coastal town and act out the film's tagline – 'Sleep all day, party all night, it's fun to be a vampire' – before being destroyed by young heroes who have swotted up on their vampire lore from comic books. But the female characters aren't invited to the party; they're either mothers or the vampire equivalent of fag hags. But these films, alongside artier, fang-free variations such as Kathryn Bigelow's vampire Western *Near Dark* (1987) and *Vampire's Kiss* (1989), in which Nicolas Cage imagines he's a vampire, eats cockroaches and terrorises his secretary, heralded a 1990s bloodsucking boom.

     A big factor in the vampire's burgeoning popularity was a new generation of post-punk teenagers influenced by the Goth and New Romantic movements, for whom the vampire was not so much a villain as a romantic role model. None of that hippy all-you-need-is-love nonsense for these consumers; they identified with these rebellious, anarchic protagonists who dressed in black and lived beyond the reach of bourgeois society. Spearheading this trend was Anne Rice's *Interview with the Vampire* (1976), which recounted its vampire protagonist's adventures in nineteenth-century Europe and New Orleans. Goth-oriented word of mouth turned the novel into a cult hit, which Rice followed up with a series of increasingly indigestible vampire chronicles. But *Interview with the Vampire* was only the first in a new wave of novels examining the psychology of vampires, who were transformed from the soulless evil creatures envisaged by Bram Stoker into dark, sometimes tormented but ineffably romantic Byronic dandies leading long and interesting lives, usually described in detailed historical flashbacks. Chelsea Quinn Yarbro's *Hotel Transylvania* (1978) and its sequels relate the adventures of the vampire Saint-Germain in ancient Rome, mediaeval France, Renaissance Italy and other historical settings. *The Vampire Tapestry* (1980) by Suzy McKee Charnas is a series of linked novellas related from the point of view of Dr Edward Lewis Weyland, vampire and anthropologist. These vampires are precursors to the vampire characters in *Buffy the Vampire Slayer*, who are not just one-dimensional monsters but complicated personalities whose histories are illuminated by flashbacks to eighteenth-century Galway, Victorian London or China during the Boxer Rebellion.

If the vampire's mutation from evil villain to romantic anti-hero robbed him of some of his bite, he was further defanged by his adaption as a loveable monster suitable for kiddy entertainment. *Sesame Street*'s The Count, Bunnicula (a vampire rabbit), Quackula (a vampire duck), Duckula (another vampire duck) and Chocula (breakfast cereal), as well as Angela Sommer-Bodenburg's *Little Vampire* books, all blunted the bloodsucker's dangerous edge while making him acceptable material for prime-time TV.

By 1992, the species was on a roll. We were already looking forward to Francis Ford Coppola's big-budget *Bram Stoker's Dracula* (1992), to John Landis applying his genre-busting know-how to *Innocent Blood* (1992), featuring a strong and principled vampire heroine who goes up against the Mafia, and to the BBC's *Vampyr – A Soap Opera* (1992), an updated London yuppie version of Heinrich Marschner's nineteenth-century opera, *Der Vampyr*. In the same year, the Canadian TV series *Forever Knight* (1992–6) featured an ancient vampire seeking redemption for his bloodsucking past (glimpsed in historical flashbacks) by working (nights, natch) as a homicide detective in present-day Toronto. Novels such as John Skipp and Craig Spector's *The Light at the End* (1986), Jim Garton's *Live Girls* (1987)

21

and Poppy Z. Brite's *Lost Souls* (1992) followed the example of *Salem's Lot* by relocating vampires in the modern world. By the 1990s, the creatures had long since transcended their origins as a folkloric myth rooted in Slav peasant superstition. They were a cultural symbol on a par with James Bond, a metaphor for capitalism, Reaganism, Thatcherism, colonialism, alienation, nihilism, anarchy, eternal youth, old age, Aids and assorted other modern malaises and maladies. They were incarnations of the *Zeitgeist*.

This was all very well. But a film called *Buffy the Vampire Slayer*? What kind of a name was Buffy, for heaven's sake?

Until 1992, the only Buffy I'd heard of had been the Native American singer–songwriter, Buffy Saint-Marie, but as a first name it struck me as being on a par with Dotty, Poppy, Daisy and other madcap types who sound as though they've escaped from the novels of Ronald Firbank or Nancy Mitford. Look it up in a dictionary, and you'll find that 'Buffy' is slang for 'intoxicated', while a 'buff' can mean 'buffet or blow'. 'To buff' is 'to shine'; the idea of 'Buffy' meaning 'shiny' (as in REM's song about 'Shiny Happy People') is irresistible, given the Slayer's Californian roots. 'Buff' is also a light brown colour (the hue of lightly tanned Californian skin?), an aficionado (as in 'film buff') or physically fit, while 'in the buff' denotes nudity, and it's true Buffy will sometimes show off her buff form in unfeasibly short skirts and midriff-revealing tops. There are echoes of 'buffo' and 'buffoon'. Best of all, for our purposes, a 'buffer' is a shield or neutralising substance. One could indeed describe Buffy Summers as a sort of supernatural shock absorber. As a name, it's more multilayered than it appears. But when I first saw it, all I thought was, 'ugh'.

Buffy the Vampire Slayer, the movie, was made for a reported $7 million – small beer by blockbuster standards (the same year's *Batman Returns* had a reported budget of $80 million), though lighting, camerawork and production design (unlike their equivalent in the later TV series) do little to camouflage the lack of funds. It's purportedly set somewhere in Los Angeles, but there's no sense of place, just a disconnected series of locations – gym, mall, park, Buffy's house, a

Buffy the Vampire Slayer: the movie

couple of anywheresville streets – and no sense at all of a community ripe for the sucking. The high-school setting seems almost incidental; we see the school grounds, meet a couple of teachers, but never get so much as a glimpse of a lesson.

Buffy, an eighteen-year-old cheerleader, was played by Kristy Swanson, an athletic-looking blonde Californian already in her twenties. As the film begins, our heroine has yet to learn that she's the Chosen One referred to in an introductory voice-over:

> Since the Dawn of Man, the Vampires have walked among us, killing, feeding. The only one with the strength or skill to stop their Heinous Evil is the Slayer, she who bears the Birthmark, the Mark of the Coven, trained by the Watcher. One Slayer dies and the next is chosen . . .

It's only when she meets a creepy older man called Merrick (Donald Sutherland) who declares he is her Watcher – the Slayer equivalent of a personal trainer – that Buffy begins her transition from ditsy blonde shopaholic to take-charge superheroine. As Buffy explores her new-found powers, she becomes alienated from her friends and instead bonds with Pike (Luke Perry of *Beverly Hills 90210* [1990–] fame), a penniless drop-out whose friend Benny has already been turned into a vampire. All over town, in fact, corpses are being found with unusual neck injuries, and only Buffy can prevent a vampire called Lothos (Rutger Hauer) and his minions from turning Los Angeles into terminal love-bite territory. The film climaxes with the vampires laying siege to the gym, where the senior dance is being held. Buffy, with Pike's help, fights them off and finally defeats Lothos.

The director was Fran Rubel Kuzui, and the screenwriter Joss Whedon. Back in 1992, his name meant nothing to me, but he already had an agenda.

> The first thing I thought of when I thought of *Buffy* – the movie – was the little blonde girl who goes into a dark alley and gets killed in every

horror movie. The idea of *Buffy* was to subvert that idea, and create someone who was a hero where she had always been a victim. That element of surprise, that element of genre-busting is very much at the heart of both the movie and the series.[3]

Alas,

It didn't turn out to be the movie that I had written. They never do, but that was my first lesson in that. Not that the movie is without merit, but I just watched a lot of stupid wannabe-star behaviour and a director with a different vision from mine – which was her right, it was her movie – but it was still frustrating.[4]

Whedon is particularly critical of Sutherland, who 'would rewrite all his dialogue, and the director would let him. He can't write – he's not a writer – so the dialogue would not make sense.' From a layman's point of view, however, it's Hauer's performance as Lothos that's the more detrimental; the actor, so chilling in psychopathic roles in *Nighthawks* (1981) and *The Hitcher* (1986), is disappointingly anaemic as the vampire villain.

Even more damaging is the uncertainty of tone, as though the film-makers couldn't decide whether they were making a teen comedy aimed at schoolkids or a straight-up vampire movie aimed at horror buffs, with the result that it works on neither level. Striking the right balance is the hardest part of making a genre hybrid, but it's not helped in the *Buffy* movie by signs of panicked editing; the film's denouement is choppy and unconvincing, with crucial pieces of business missing, resulting in a limp anti-climax just when we should be revving up to the best prom conflagration since *Carrie*.

In Whedon's original screenplay (traces of which survive in Richie Tankersley Cusick's novelisation, as well as in the graphic novel *The Origin*), Buffy ends up burning down the gym – an event that never made it into the finished film, though it's referred to more than once in

25

the TV series. But at the time of the film's UK release in 1992, the series wasn't even a twinkle in Joss Whedon's eye. Like most film critics, I relegated the movie to an also-ran in my review column, in third place behind Woody Allen's *Husbands and Wives* and Ridley Scott's *1942 – Conquest of Paradise*. That was it, I thought, just a lame horror comedy. Nice idea, shame about the execution.

3 Welcome to the Hellmouth

What Happens in Season One

Buffy Summers and her mother, Joyce, have just moved to the small American town of Sunnydale from Los Angeles, where Buffy was expelled from school for burning down the gym. Buffy is keen to start afresh and leave vampire slaying behind her, but on her first day at Sunnydale High School she runs into the librarian, an Englishman called Rupert Giles, who introduces himself as her Watcher and informs her that Sunnydale is situated on a 'Hellmouth' and is thus rife with vampire and other demonic activity. Buffy tells him she's not interested, but after the discovery of a corpse in a school locker her Slayer instincts take over.

Buffy's good looks and fashion sense impress the class bitch, Cordelia Chase, but Cordelia is soon alienated by the new girl's willingness to hang out with the class nerds, Xander Harris and Willow Rosenberg. Willow has been Xander's friend since childhood, and is secretly in love with him; he in his turn develops an unrequited crush on Buffy, who fails dismally in her attempts to date normal boys while finding herself increasingly attracted to Angel, a mysterious but attractive stranger who turns out to be a vampire with a soul, seeking redemption for past sins. Meanwhile, bookish Giles is attracted to Jenny

Calendar, a 'techno-pagan' who teaches computer studies. Xander, Willow and, ultimately, Cordelia find out about Buffy's secret identity and, in the course of the season, help her tackle assorted demons and monsters, including hyena people who eat the school's head, Principal Flutie. His replacement is the short, despotic Principal Snyder.

In Season One the chief villain – or 'Big Bad' – is the Master, an ancient vampire trapped beneath the school, who is planning to escape and open the Hellmouth, thus bringing about the End of the World. In the final episode of the season, he kills Buffy, but Xander revives her with CPR, and she goes on to destroy the Master and (for the first but not the last time) save the world.

There is on the Internet a website called 'Accounts of how Buffy Followers came to watch the show'.[5] It's remarkable how many fans feel compelled to describe in detail the circumstances of that first discovery, much as people remember what they were doing when they heard President Kennedy had been shot or that Princess Diana had been killed in a car crash. The discovery of *Buffy the Vampire Slayer* was, for its fans, nothing short of a life-changing experience.

My own discovery was not a case of love at first sight. It was more like one of those love affairs in which initial indifference segues into casual interest followed by a belated realisation that one has actively been seeking out the loved one's company. When I first spotted *Buffy the Vampire Slayer* in the TV schedules, I paused just long enough to wonder why anyone had bothered to produce a spin-off of a naff film that as far as I was aware hadn't even inspired a cult following. There has never been any shortage of TV series spawned by hit films (*The Odd Couple* [1967], *Fame* [1980], *Dirty Dancing* [1987]) or even minor cults (*Highlander* [1986], *Nikita* [1990]), but there are also, more bafflingly, TV spin-offs of films that were neither massive hits nor cults (*Blue Thunder* [1982], *Parenthood*, *The Net* [1995]) and *Buffy the Vampire Slayer* seemed to fall into the latter category. When one of my friends suggested it was worth a look and that the heroine's vampire boyfriend, in particular, was hot, I didn't heed her advice. Besides, it was being shown on Saturday evenings, when any self-respecting person would be out on the town. When, finally, I did catch an episode, it was halfway through the second season: a robot version of *Bluebeard* in which Buffy accidentally kills her mother's new beau, though luckily for her he turns out to be not a human but an android with a serial wife habit. It was amusing enough, though I was less than impressed by the famous vampire boyfriend, who struck me as listless (what I didn't know was that he'd had most of his blood drained in a previous episode). Apart from a graveyard scene when Buffy takes out her resentment of her mom's new squeeze on the newly risen undead, there was a disappointing lack of *vampire* action. Hah, I sneered, they might as well have called it *Buffy the Robot Slayer*.

The only cast member I'd heard of was guest star John Ritter, who played Ted the Robot. But there were two vaguely familiar faces. The first was Buffy's Watcher, Giles, played by English actor Anthony Stewart Head, best known for a series of 1980s Gold Blend commercials in which instant coffee acted like Spanish Fly on him and his neighbour. The second vaguely familiar face belonged to the perky blonde actress playing Buffy, Sarah Michelle Gellar, but it wasn't until afterwards that I worked out I'd already seen her in the slasher movie *I Know What You Did Last Summer* (1997), in which she'd met the inevitable fate of all perky blonde actresses in such movies – she panicked, screamed and was hacked to pieces, a perfect example of Whedon's 'little blonde girl who goes into a dark alley and gets killed'. Gellar would shortly be meeting a similar fate in *Scream 2* (1997). I failed dismally to notice that *Buffy the Vampire Slayer* was already turning this hoary old cliché on its head.

Gellar was spotted by a talent agent at the age of four, made her first film at the age of six and, by the time she was cast as Buffy, was a teenage veteran with a solid track record in commercials and TV soaps, notably a two-year stint on *All My Children* (1970–). But compared to Kristy Swanson in the movie, Gellar seemed to me skinny verging on anorexic, her prettiness marred by a weak chin and a whiny voice. She reminded me of an animated Barbie doll. (Years later, when I saw her in the flesh at a critics' preview of the film *Cruel Intentions*

[1999], I was struck by her petiteness; at 5'3" she was only an inch shorter than me, but so fine-boned that she made me feel like a galumphing elephant – and it's not as though I'm large.) But she handled herself well in the action scenes (it was years before I twigged she had a stunt double), and struck a deft balance between stupid and smart, and by the end of that first episode I was forced to admit she was a better Buffy than Swanson had ever been.

But there was nothing in that first experience to suggest that Buffy Summers might be the action heroine for whom I'd been searching all my life, and I didn't bother to watch the next episode. Apparently I wasn't the only one with better things to do on a Saturday night; due to poor ratings, Sky One unceremoniously pulled the series off air a few weeks later.

Buffy Summers: Vampire Slayer

It wasn't until BBC2 started broadcasting *Buffy the Vampire Slayer* on a weekday, directly after *Star Trek: The Next Generation* (1987–), that I realised what I'd been missing. To begin with, ours wasn't an easy relationship: between 1998 and 2000 Buffy stood me up no fewer than fourteen times as the BBC peremptorily replaced her with snooker or darts. But by the time Sky One started repeating Season Two in a regular Friday-night slot, and then followed it up with Season Three, I was diligently setting up the video recorder every week. Soon I was setting up two separate video recorders, just to be on the safe side. And that was it; I was hooked. And I stuck by Buffy for better and for worse, even after I moved to France and had to rely on the goodwill of friends who taped or downloaded each new episode for me. I stayed faithful to the end.

Buffy the Vampire Slayer, the series, was commissioned by Warner Brothers as a mid-season replacement for an Aaron Spelling-produced soap opera called *Savannah* (1996–7). Thus, the first season ran for only twelve episodes, which allowed Joss Whedon and his collaborators enough time to establish the characters, format and ground rules (and even gave them the opportunity for a few reshoots), without needing to pad the concept out to a quality-sapping twenty-two episodes. In fact, in terms of the *Buffy* canon, Season One stands alone; the potential is there for further development, but it's remarkably self-sufficient.

    'Welcome to the Hellmouth' is both an introduction for newcomers and, by taking up more or less where the movie left off, a plunge *in medias res* for those already familiar with the 1992 film, hitherto consigned to backstory, though there are a few minor discrepancies between movie and series. In the film, Buffy is eighteen years old, but as the series begins she has regressed to sixteen. Buffy's mom is no longer a flighty dope but solicitous Joyce (a metamorphosis that could conceivably be explained by her having split up with Buffy's dad in the interim). In the film, Buffy gets abdominal cramps whenever there's a vampire in the vicinity ('My secret weapon is PMS'), but this conceit is dropped for the series, and it's true it might have worn a little thin over seven seasons, with the heroine continually forced to pause in mid-battle to clutch her stomach or swallow painkillers. But thanks to the backstory, when we meet the Buffy of the series she already has a secret identity at odds with her appearance and behaviour. She's already intriguing.

Buffy will form the hub of the 'Core Four' – the four central characters who will stick together, more or less, for seven seasons. The other three are Giles, Willow and Xander, introduced as stereotypes but fleshed out as the series progresses. Giles is the first but not the last British character (Whedon took 'A' levels at Winchester College, in the UK) and steps into Merrick's shoes as Buffy's Watcher, the Man with the Knowledge. He will be her mentor, guide and father figure. If this

Buffy's Watcher, Rupert Giles

were a Hammer vampire movie, Giles would be Van Helsing – sage, vampire hunter, maybe even the hero – but by the standards of a series aimed at teenage viewers he's over the hill. Though Giles acquits himself well in the action scenes (as befits a classically trained Englishman, he's particularly handy with a sword), his primary function is to leaf through dusty tomes and provide the series with most of its expository dialogue about demons, arcane hexes and ancient artefacts. In short, much of his dialogue is gobbledygook (or 'phlebotinin', as the writers started calling it), though Anthony Stewart Head's experience in presenting instant coffee as a sexy and exciting beverage must come in useful when he's required to sell dialogue such as, 'On rare occasions, inanimate objects of human quality such as dolls or mannequins, already mystically possessed of consciousness, have acted upon their desire to be human by harvesting organs.' Or incantations such as, 'Let the darkness shine, cover us with holy fear. Show me. Corsheth and Gilail, the gate is closed . . .' One suspects that, to Americans, such pronouncements sound more convincing when delivered in an English accent, and indeed Giles is a misguided American idea of a typical Englishman – a stuffy young fogey (forty-ish) in spectacles and tweed, with a slight stutter and marked antipathy towards teen culture and new-fangled things like computers. His pompousness is also a useful device for the younger characters to prove how hip, witty and irreverent they are, and so his portentous pronouncements are always being undercut. When Giles advises Buffy to hone her mystic senses so she will be able to sense the presence of vampires, for example, she responds by immediately recognising a nearby vampire by his outmoded fashion sense. 'Trust me, only someone living underground for ten years would think that was still the look.'

33

Sunnydale High, like any American high school worthy of the name, is a hotbed of cliques such as cheerleaders, jocks and geeks. Cordelia, a bitchy cheerleader type with a vacuous, self-centred, shopping-mad personality not unlike that of Buffy herself at the beginning of the 1992 movie, sets Buffy a coolness test (black nail polish? James Spader? frappacino?) which Buffy passes with flying

Cordelia Chase, class bitch

colours, but Cordelia recoils when Buffy refuses to follow her example and snub the class geeks. It's a measure of how much the Slayer has already been changed by her vampire-slaying experiences; she yearns to fit in, but despite her cheerleader looks, instinctively grasps that she has more in common with the geeky outsiders than with the cool cliquesters. From a viewer's point of view, she's the best of both worlds – a geek in a gorgeous body, a social outcast in pretty blonde wrapping.

She's also a reminder that being an outsider doesn't automatically preclude having friends and belonging to your own exclusive clique, even if you have to invent it yourself. 'You're the Slayer,' Willow says to Buffy, 'and we're, like, the Slayerettes.'

Buffy, Giles, Willow and Xander band together to form a secret society in the honourable tradition of clandestine crime-fighting bands such as the Famous Five or the Secret Seven. They even adopt a name, 'The Scooby Gang', a reference to the cartoon series *Scooby Doo Where Are You!* (1969–70) and abbreviated in later episodes to 'The Scoobies'. Scoobies will come and go – Angel, Cordelia, Oz, Anya, Riley, Tara, Spike and Dawn will all chip in at various points – but it's only the Core Four who stay the course.

'Welcome to the Hellmouth' begins with a teenage couple breaking into Sunnydale High School at night. We've already been primed, by the title of the show and the conventions of pre-credits sequences, for something shocking to happen, and it duly does, though not in the way we expect. The girl, maybe a little too old to pass as a teenager but dressed in a cute

Welcome to the Hellmouth: Darla prepares to take a bite out of her date

approximation of school uniform with a short plaid skirt, is blonde and timid. (School uniform is not compulsory in most American high schools, allowing Buffy and her friends to flaunt a new outfit in every episode. It's never explained how a single mother like Joyce manages to bankroll her daughter's non-stop fashion parade out of what can hardly be an enormous salary from her job in an art gallery.) The blonde is traditional victim material, in other words. The boy is older and more confident, and appears to be luring her into a situation where he can prey on her, possibly sexually but more likely (that title again) by sinking his fangs into her neck . . .

Joss Whedon: 'Anyone who's well-versed in horror movies know what's going to happen in this scene, and the idea is always to try and surprise them, to subvert the obvious.'[6]

And so it's not the guy, but the *girl* who suddenly morphs into a bumpy-faced monster and sinks her fangs into his neck. Had I watched this episode before the others, as intended, this reversal of expectations would in itself have been sufficient to pique my curiosity. According to Whedon, it illustrates the mission statement of the show: 'Nothing Is As It Seems'.[7] (Nothing is as it seems, indeed; the girl vampire is Darla, who in later episodes of *Buffy the Vampire Slayer* and its spin-off series *Angel* will develop an entire history and character traits that aren't even hinted at here, but then she was initially intended to be a one-off – in the unaired pilot she was staked.)

And we're plunged into the credit sequence, a fast-moving montage of forthcoming highlights from the season set to instrumental music by Nerf Herder (named after Princess Leia's insult to Han Solo in *The Empire Strikes Back* [1980]: 'Why, you stuck-up, half-witted, scruffy-looking nerf herder') which blasts apart the stately gothic-sounding organ introduction (at the same time as images of ancient-looking Germanic text get blasted apart by the action montage) with a pounding four-chord punk-rock-à-la-sauce-metal riff. 'This is a girl', says Joss Whedon, 'who refuses to be in a horror movie.'[8]

Buffy the Vampire Slayer has begun.

Whedon says, 'We picked and chose our vampire lore based on lots of different myths – *Dracula*, *The Lost Boys*, everything we'd seen – we took whatever we wanted.'[9] Some of the decisions were pragmatic; for example, whenever vampires are staked, they and their clothes immediately disintegrate – a process referred to throughout the series as 'dusting'. On Whedon's part, it provided a handy solution to what might have been a problem in a show with a big body count. 'I didn't think it would be fun to have fifteen minutes of Let's Clean Up the Bodies.'[10] Hence vampires, and also many of the demons, have a helpful tendency to disappear ('No fuss, no muss,' says Buffy) or dissolve into puddles of goo. The first episode also deals swiftly with the perennial genre problem, 'This may be the dumb question, but shouldn't we call the police?' The answer is no: the police wouldn't understand . . . No-one ever proposes it again, though Giles does comment at the end of Season Two, 'In case you haven't noticed, the police in Sunnydale are deeply stupid.' (Not only that, but as the series progresses, there are hints that the authorities, whether from blind ignorance or active malice, are actually in cahoots with evil.) And why didn't the vampires fly or turn into bats, like they do in *Dracula* or *The Lost Boys*? Answer – not enough budget.

As well as the Core Four and Cordelia, 'Welcome to the Hellmouth' also introduces us to Angel, a tall dark stranger who hovers enigmatically on the sidelines but lends Buffy a hand when the going gets tough. He's so tall, dark and handsome, in fact, there's no question he will be providing serious romantic interest in the near future – otherwise, what would his purpose be? To begin with, Buffy is annoyed by his habit of popping up unexpectedly, but it's obvious to anyone familiar with romantic movie conventions that annoyance will change to attraction, and so it proves. When, in the seventh episode, she and Angel finally get down to serious snogging manoeuvres, he reacts violently to the accidental touch of her crucifix and she discovers what we've suspected all along – that he's a vampire.

Ah, but not just any old vampire. This is a 241-year-old vampire whose soul has been restored by a gypsy curse, leaving him

37

Buffy and Angel

tormented by the memory of all the atrocities his demon self has
committed. So even though he has regular vampire habits (doesn't care
for sunlight or crucifixes, possesses superstrength, can't enter a private
house without invitation) he is now operating on the side of the good
guys, seeking redemption. The inclusion of a major recurring vampire
character who is not one of the bad guys is a smart move, not just
hinting at the potential for recidivism and redemption, not just
providing an excuse for historical flashbacks, not just providing a
potential identification figure for all the brooding Goths in the audience
who may find Buffy's cheerleading blondeness just too cute to stomach,
but also providing a great many opportunities for the writers to make
jokes about the drawbacks of dating an older guy. 'You're, like, 224
years older than I am,' marvels Buffy at one point.

Angel in vamp-face

When I first saw the vampires in *Buffy the Vampire Slayer* I was disappointed. For me, part of the creatures' appeal has always been their physical resemblance to humans. They're the aristocrats – literally so in the case of Count Dracula – of the supernatural world. Unlike werewolves and zombies, they can hold a civilised conversation and their feeding is relatively dainty, leaving just two neat little holes in the neck. Unlike werewolves and zombies, they can be seductive, and most victims would probably opt to be bitten by a charismatic person in a cape rather than a rotting lunkhead which looks as though it might have rabies. In Seasons Two and Three of *Buffy the Vampire Slayer*, Willow has a relationship with a werewolf (Oz), but this gets put on hold whenever the moon is full; it's the human whom she dates, kisses and (eventually) has sex with, not his hairy alter ego, and Oz spends his time of the month (when his bestial urges would undoubtedly prove too much for a schoolgirl to handle) behind bars. In terms of human–monster miscegenation, it's only really the vampire who holds out any potential.

The first important movie vampire wasn't sexy at all; Count Orlock in *Nosferatu* (1922) is a horrible hairless walking corpse with pointy fangs, long fingernails and sunken eyes, but until the 1980s, most vampires tended to look pretty normal. Bela Lugosi's *Dracula* (1930) is rendered sinister not through monster make-up but by shadowy lighting, the actor's heavy Slavic accent and facial features – the archetypal dodgy European, in other words. In Hammer's *Dracula* (1957) and its sequels, Christopher Lee's transformation into a blood-sucking fiend is marked by nothing more radical than red contact lenses and fangs. In Hammer's vampire movies, in fact, the vampires are invariably sexier than the dry old coves who hunt them down.

But in 1981, two werewolf movies (*An American Werewolf in London* and *The Howling*) revolutionised the horror genre with their scenes of men and women metamorphosing into hairy beasts before our very eyes. Cinema would never be the same again; why settle for sinister shadows and contact lenses when there's a whole special-effects crew out there, ready to rustle up a full-blown transformation sequence with pulsating condoms, life-size models and (later) computer-generated imagery? And so in films like *Fright Night*, *Vamp* and *The Lost Boys*, vampires developed a full case of special effects-itis, morphing whenever the bloodlust took them into bumpy-faced monsters who inevitably succumbed in the final reel to a *Sturm und Drang* of pyrotechnic meltdown into multicoloured goo, the latter probably inspired by the cheap and cheerful zombie splatter of *The Evil Dead* (1983).

Buffy the Vampire Slayer took its cue from the monstrous-looking vampires of these films, rather than subtler variations on the myth such as *Near Dark*, which dispenses with fangs, if not with pyrotechnics (the vampire characters tend to ignite whenever sunlight hits them). The vampires in *Buffy the Vampire Slayer* look human enough until they need to feed or fight, when they morph into 'vamp-face' – a bumpy, mongoloid forehead that completely ruins what they might have had in the way of an elegant profile, fangs that seem too big for their mouths (giving most of the vampires slight speech impediments) and squinty orange eyes. Not a pretty sight.

Whedon, however, had a sound enough reason for this policy.

> The decision to make vamp-face for the vampires was very conscious and very thought out . . . Because when Buffy is fighting them it was important to me that they look like aliens, monsters . . . I didn't want to put a show on the air about a high-school student who was stabbing normal-looking people in the heart. I thought somehow that might send out the wrong message. But when they are clearly monsters it takes it to a level of fantasy that is safer.[11]

Well yes. I was being selfish. I hadn't taken into account that it was a TV show aimed principally at adolescents and that – disturbing though it manages to be at times – there could be no way on earth the network would allow it to be *too* outrageous, like the Japanese film *Battle Royale* (2000), which includes scenes of normal-looking schoolchildren going Peckinpah on each other with crossbows and machine-guns. *Buffy the Vampire Slayer*, despite all the condemnation heaped upon its head by Christians ('This program is a direct offense to God and his commandments')[12] and the Parents Television Council ('Buffy ranks number one on the worst list because of its graphic violence and sex, often mixing the two with an underlying occultist element'),[13] is a very moralistic series. Evil may sometimes gain temporary ascendancy, but it never triumphs. Buffy Summers was designed by Whedon to be a positive female role model. With such a pedagogic agenda, it would never do to make the evil characters appear too glamorous, and the bumpy vamp-face is certainly off-putting. For me, not wanting to look like that would in itself be motivation enough to avoid becoming a vampire.

The recurring villain in Season One is the Master, an ancient and powerful Orlock lookalike in a black PVC Mao suit. The Master

41

Stuck in ugly mode: the Master

is so old he's got stuck in ugly mode – we never find out what he looked like before he was a vampire, and we don't get peeks into his past, as we do with other major vampire characters later on. Unlike most of the younger vampires, he has hypnotic powers, which he uses on Buffy just before chowing down on her neck in the season finale. His aims are a) to escape (which is understandable, since he appears to lead a rather boring life underground, surrounded by dim-witted minions) and b) to open the Hellmouth, thus bringing about the End of the World, though this would presumably deprive him of his primary food source. He's the first but not the last vampire to try and bring about the End of the World, though at the end of Season Two, the vampire Spike will buck this trend by striking a deal with Buffy to *prevent* the apocalypse. 'You've got dog racing, Manchester United and you've got people,' he explains. 'Billions of people, walking around like Happy Meals with legs.'

Unlike the Master, Angel in non-vamp mode is a hunk, and while I failed to share my girlfriends' enthusiasm for someone who was so shamelessly tall, dark and broody, his drawing power on the female audience was unquestionable, while one should never underestimate the physical charms of Buffy, Cordelia and even geeky Willow in helping the series appeal to the young male demographic. But gorgeous-looking actors aren't exactly hard to find on American TV. What made *Buffy the Vampire Slayer* click with viewers was the writing. The secret of the show's success is a sort of sleight of writer's hand. It was initially presented as a series of demon-of-the-week episodes, with Buffy and her chums confronted each week by a different monster. In Season One, alongside the omnipresent vampires, the monsters included witches, insect women, hyena people and an invisible girl. In a typical episode, the monster hurts or even kills someone and threatens to add a member of the Scooby Gang to its score before finally being defeated by Buffy and the gang.

Fantasy genres are frequently dimissed by high-minded critics as escapist and unrealistic, but for young people weaned on an irony-laden culture in which the only acceptable reaction is cynicism, they provide a useful way of embracing life-or-death emotions, fears and desires too painful or embarrassing or frightening to contemplate in a reality-based genre. The vampires and demons and monsters in *Buffy the Vampire Slayer* are often adolescent fears made 'real', as in 'The Pack', in which a clique of delinquent students are possessed by the predatory spirits of hyenas which make them act even more sociopathically than usual, or 'Out of Mind, Out of Sight', which features a girl so ignored by her classmates that she literally becomes invisible. But though individual episodes don't require insider knowledge, and are generally self-contained in terms of closure, there are also, running through them at an almost subliminal level, threads that tie characters and themes into longer story arcs that play out over the course of a season, such as Buffy and Angel's growing attraction for each other, or Buffy's developing friendship with the Scoobies and relationship with her mother, or the ever-growing menace of the Big Bad, or – the thread that binds all seven seasons together – Buffy's realisation of what it means to be a superhero.

That's writing as in structure or narrative, but there's also the dialogue, so funny and idiosyncratic that entire websites and even an OUP dictionary have been dedicated to it. The Scoobies' conversation is peppered with references to cult TV shows and films: *The Wild Bunch*, *The Exorcist*, *Godzilla*, *The Shining*, *Spider-Man*, *Star Trek*, *Lost in Space*, *The Untouchables*, *Superman*, *Sabrina the Teenage Witch* are just some of the titles casually dropped into Season One. And the name-dropping is not just limited to quotes, as in Buffy's 'My spider-sense is tingling!' but twisted into adjectives and verbs. 'We're talking full-on *Exorcist* twist,' says Buffy, describing a teacher's head doing a 360-degree spin, while Xander asks, 'Does anyone else here feel Keyser Soze'd?', referring to the criminal mastermind from *The Usual Suspects* (1995).

Buffyspeak, though it can sometimes include a few lines in alien or demon tongue, is not a perfectly conceived language like the Elvish, Dwarvish or Entish in J.R.R. Tolkien's *The Lord of the Rings*, or the Klingon lingo invented by Marc Okrand for *Star Trek*. It has more in common with Newspeak in George Orwell's *Nineteen Eighty-Four*, with its modification of existing words to create new formations ('goodthinkful', 'doubleplus good') or Nadsat in Anthony Burgess's *A Clockwork Orange*, with its Russian-derived slang words ('horrorshow', 'millicents'). Buffy language is sprinkled with neologisms built from regular words or names customised by prefixes such as un- (undead, ungood, unbad) or über (überBuffy, übervampire) and suffixes such as -age (slayage, suckage, kissage) or -y (frowny, huntery, judgy, murdery). Or it's simply a droll way with words, as in Xander's observation that 'every woman in Sunnydale wants to make me her cuddle-monkey', or Cordelia's comment when she first lays eyes on Angel – 'Hello, salty goodness!'

The wonder is that with so many different writers providing stories and dialogue the Buffyverse is such a cohesive, coherent place. But then, as Jane Espenson wrote in her preface to *Slayer Slang*, 'The only thing that gives us coherence is that . . . we're all doing our darnedest to do a Joss Whedon impersonation.'[14]

4 Love and Other Catastrophes

What Happens in Season Two

Several important new players arrive in Sunnydale. Spike and Drusilla are a groovy English vampire couple: he's a punk with bleached blond hair and a rebellious attitude; she's psychic, stark raving mad and physically frail after a run-in with a mob in Prague. Halfway through the season, after a set-to with the Scoobies, their roles are reversed: Dru recovers her health and Spike ends up in a wheelchair. We are also introduced to Kendra, a gung-ho but endearingly naïve Jamaican Slayer who was 'activated' when Buffy died (briefly) at the hands of the Master at the end of Season One. It's patiently explained to Kendra that Angel, although a vampire, is one of the good guys, and is therefore not to be killed.

In the course of the season, Buffy confronts and defeats assorted demons-of-the-week, including an Inca mummy-girl, a snake god worshipped by wealthy frat boys, a Bezoar demon whose eggs hatch mind-controlling parasites, Joyce's evil robot boyfriend, the ghosts of a teacher and pupil who re-enact the same murder–suicide over and over again and Halloween costumes that turn those wearing them into literal incarnations of their disguises. Xander and Cordelia, despite mutual antipathy, embark on a clandestine relationship that involves a lot of fooling around in dark cupboards; they're eventually discovered by Willow. She's naturally devastated ('You'd rather be with someone you hate than with me') but finds consolation with Oz, a laid-back guitarist with the band Dingoes Ate My Baby. Oz also happens to be a werewolf, who has to be locked in a cage every full moon so he won't kill anyone.

Oz is not the only character to have a dark secret. In his youth, Giles was a tearaway delinquent, known to his friends as 'Ripper', who dabbled in black magic. Jenny turns out to be a descendant of the gypsies who cursed Angel, and has been sent to Sunnydale to keep an eye on him. Meanwhile, Angel and Buffy have fallen deeply in love, and on Buffy's seventeenth birthday they finally have sex; unfortunately, this provides Angel with a moment of true happiness that – as per the rules of the curse – deprives him of his soul and makes him revert to his evil vampire self, known as Angelus. He promptly forms a *ménage-à-trois* with his old pals Spike and Dru (though Spike is ambivalent; he and Angelus have always been rivals) and the three of them resurrect a powerful creature called the Judge, who starts sucking the souls out of shoppers at the Sunnydale Mall until Buffy settles his hash with a rocket launcher. Angelus continues to make her life a misery, and kills Jenny (who has been working on a spell to restore his soul) and taunts Giles with the corpse. Giles responds with a solo attack on vampire HQ, but ends up having to be rescued by Buffy.

Joyce witnesses her first dusting and has trouble adjusting to the discovery that her daughter is the Slayer. In the course of yet another plan to bring about the End of the World, Dru kills Kendra and the cops attempt to arrest Buffy for the murder; she goes on the run, though not before Principal Snyder has expelled her from school. Spike (who has recovered the use of his legs) agrees to help the Scoobies in exchange for being allowed to leave Sunnydale with Dru. Willow casts a spell to restore Angel's soul, but Xander fails to tell Buffy, who is forced to kill her lover in order to prevent the End of the World. Shattered by events, she catches the bus out of town.

47

The recent history of American television is littered with the corpses of series that have been terminated by the networks that spawned them. It's a particularly vicious sort of cultural eugenics; rarely is a show allowed time to find its feet. Sometimes the plug is pulled mid-season, occasionally it's yanked after only a few episodes have been aired. For every *Beverly Hills 90210*, which was allowed to dribble on for ten seasons, there's a *My So-Called Life* (1995), which, despite having been adored by critics and viewers, was snuffed out after a single season. For every *Alias* (in its fourth season at the time of writing) there's a *Wonderfalls* (2004), peremptorily axed after only four of its thirteen episodes had been aired. If a new series has the bad luck to be scheduled at the same time as a well-established show with big ratings, its days are inevitably numbered. Quality is no guarantee of survival; it's a cut-throat cathode world, a brutal Darwinian struggle in which only the strongest survive. Enthusiastic reviews and a loyal fan base are not enough; it's ratings that count. Even a strong track record counts for nothing; Joss Whedon may have been the celebrated creator of *Buffy the Vampire Slayer* and its spin-off, *Angel*, two shows with fanatical followings and cultural influence far beyond the target demographic, but it didn't stop the network from murdering his new baby, *Firefly*, before its first season had run its course. Of course, it didn't help that episodes were aired in the wrong order.

So how did *Buffy the Vampire Slayer* manage to last seven seasons, surviving major timeslot changes and even, in its final two seasons, a change of network? If we knew the answer to that, we'd all be successful TV writers, but the basic formula is a uniquely flexible one. Vampires and demons and monsters are all very well, and lots of fun, but a series cannot extend to 144 episodes (that's ninety-six hours, the equivalent of sixty-four ninety-minute movies) on a demon-of-the-week and sparkling dialogue alone.

The real meat in the case of *Buffy the Vampire Slayer* is character, or, more to the point, character change. 'Change is a mandate on the show,'[15] says Whedon. The characters can't stand still; they have to keep developing. 'That's one of the realities of high school,' says

Whedon (though he might just as well be talking about life). 'Nobody is what they are forever. They change, their alliances change and sometimes dissolve.'[16] And so, week after week in Whedon's slowly unfolding masterplan, familiar characters reveal hidden depths, dark secrets or form new and unexpected alliances as, piece by piece, the mythology of the Buffyverse falls into place. 'We're not good at writing *The X-Files*, horror stories our people are peripheral to,' Whedon once said *à propos* of *Angel*. 'We're good at writing the stories of our people.'[17]

Buffy may be the title character, the kick-ass action heroine for whom I was waiting all my life, but the series is more than just a study in whizz-bang heroics. It's also a portrait in how an action hero or heroine can be successfully integrated into society and relate to other people as opposed to standing alone and aloof, how the emotional ties of family and friends can make her stronger, not weaker. According to the Buffyverse, past Slayers have all been loners, operating clandestinely, without family or friends – as per the introductory voice-over in the early seasons – 'She alone will stand against the vampires, the demons and the forces of darkness.' Buffy is expected to follow in this tradition and, to begin with, it seems as though Willow and Xander, who share her secret but not her superpowers, are going to be millstones around her neck; at best they will cramp her style, at worst they will place her in jeopardy by getting into trouble and having to be rescued. This is indeed one of the narrative functions of the Scoobies in Season One. Week after week, Buffy proves she can deal with any monster the writers throw at her, but barely an episode goes by in which one of her friends doesn't end up being threatened with some hideous fate; Xander has to be rescued before he can be raped and decapitated by a preying she-mantis; Giles has to be rescued before he can be guillotined by an organ-harvesting demon with designs on his brain; Willow has to be rescued from an online relationship with the demon, Moloch; Cordelia has to be rescued from an invisible girl who threatens to disfigure her (obviously a fate worse than death where Cordelia is concerned). Whedon says

49

> One of the biggest problems with the show is that your heroine . . . is stronger than a lot of the things she faces, she's take-charge . . . And creating opportunities for her to be in genuine peril [is] difficult because the whole point is her strength, so it's very good to have the ancillary characters, especially because . . . they sometimes actually get killed, and really stress their vulnerability.[18]

Of the Core Four, it's Willow who changes most dramatically. In Season One, she's a nerd. In Seasons Two and Three, she's a nerd with a groovy boyfriend (Oz) and dabbles in magic. In Season Four, she loses the groovy boyfriend, acquires a girlfriend (Tara) and more magic skill. In Season Five, she shows flashes of scary magic power and in Season Six,

Willow models 'the softer side of Sears'

becomes addicted to it, tries to go cold turkey, ends up out of control, kills people and – why not? all the other villains are doing it – tries to bring about the End of the World. In Season Seven, she's a subdued recovering addict who finds another girlfriend to replace the one who died, before finally finding a way of harnessing her magic power to do good instead of evil.

The name Willow is a fitting combination of droopy (like the tree) and strong (as in Will, which is what Xander sometimes calls her). According to Celtic lunar astrology, not only was willow bark used to conjure spirits, but the words 'witchcraft' and 'wicca' are actually derived from the word 'willow'. In an unaired pilot for Season One, Willow was played by Riff Regan, a shy-looking, sweet-faced and decidedly unwillowy actress. She looks more of a geek than her replacement, Alyson Hannigan, could ever be. Hannigan acts geeky, but still has the sort of figure that can get her included (alongside the show's other actresses) in *FHM*'s annual poll of 100 Sexiest Women. After watching seven seasons of Hannigan fully in charge of Willow's changing looks, sexual preferences and blossoming witchy talent, it's hard to imagine what Regan would have made of the character if she'd been kept on, and there's nothing in the actress's subsequent career (a couple of guest slots in other TV shows, a couple of TV movies) to suggest that reassignment of the role was a mistake. Riff Regan is to *Buffy the Vampire Slayer* what Pete Best was to the Beatles – an also-ran who fell by the wayside at an early stage and missed out on iconic status.

Of the casting of Willow, Whedon says, 'I was determined that we didn't have the Supermodel in hornrims.'[19] In 'Welcome to the Hellmouth', Hannigan certainly dresses the part ('the softer side of Sears' as Cordelia bitchily describes it) in dorky pinafore frock, unflattering white tights and droopy hair. (It's useful, of course, that she's a redhead, and thus easily distinguishable from blonde Buffy and brunette Cordelia. One of my many problems with *Charmed* is that I've always had trouble telling the three dark-haired actresses apart – and it doesn't help that their names all begin with P, as in Phoebe, Piper, Pru, Paige, Poopy, what have you.) Even so, the network demanded that

51

Willow look more fashionable in subsequent episodes, so the 'softer side of Sears' devolves into a more bohemian, floaty, neo-hippy dress sense, leaving Hannigan having to convey geekiness by delivering her dialogue like someone who thinks faster than she talks, out of breath and needlessly wordy. With her widow's peak, wide eyes and over-expressive face she frequently reminds me of a clown, though since (like Xander) I find clowns sinister, this doesn't endear her to me. The problem with geeks is that their self-esteem has often taken such a battering that they spend most of their time apologising. Sometimes, Willow takes so long to come out with the simplest remark that you want to slap her, but Hannigan manages, just, to keep her on the bearable side of annoying, though she does sometimes come very close to crossing the line, particularly after hooking up with Tara in Season Four.

It wasn't until I watched a dubbed-into-French episode of *Buffy contre les vampires*, in which Xander is referred to throughout as 'Alex' that I finally realised (duh) that Xander is short for Alexander. If Alexander is the name of a conquering hero, then Xander (*ou Alex, si vous voulez*) is only half a hero. Of all the main characters, he's the only one who never gets to wield supernatural powers, and his progress through the series is less melodramatic than that of Buffy or Willow. He never seems threatened by the fact that Buffy is stronger, smarter and more important in the cosmic scheme of things than he is; on the contrary, he's rather turned on by it. In Season One, he's a nerd with a crush on Buffy. In Seasons Two and Three, he's a nerd with a love–hate relationship with Cordelia, has a one-night stand with Faith and attracts the attention of ex-demon Anya. In Season Four, he's an unqualified school-leaver struggling to find his place in the world, but his relationship with Anya deepens until, in Season Five, they get engaged. In Season Six, he finds his niche in the world of work as a construction site foreman, and realises at the eleventh hour that he's not ready to get married. In Season Seven, it's as though the writers have run out of things for him to do (he doesn't even appear in the key episode

'Conversations with Dead People', the season's Big Bad evidently concluding that he's not enough of a threat to send a dead person for him to converse with) and he does little but make wisecracks and give pep talks and repair a lot of smashed windows until losing an eye to the Big Bad (the one-eyed Cyclops of Greek mythology are known, like Xander, for their construction work), after which he has sex with Anya again, just before she's killed in the final battle. He's cut up about her death, but we never find out just how much, because it's there that the series ends.

Whedon admits Xander is the character with whom he particularly identified (though this isn't much of a stretch, since all the other mains are either female, English or vampires). Xander is goofy,

53

Xander: 'Looking at linoleum makes me want to have sex'

self-deprecating and sex-obsessed (Cordelia: 'Does looking at guns make you want to have sex?' Xander: 'I'm seventeen. Looking at linoleum makes me want to have sex'). He gets tongue-tied in the presence of pretty girls, but in fact, Xander appears so witty, funny and attractive to viewers at home – and in 'Go Fish', in which he joins the swimming team, he looks so very fit in his Speedos – it's a wonder he's not the most popular guy in the class, instead of a despised geek. 'He's a lot prettier and more muscular than anyone who acts like that should be,' says Whedon, 'but this is television, so get over it.'[20]

In fact Xander is such an idealised nerd that he's not a nerd at all, though the other characters – and indeed the show's writers – don't seem to notice that, and the show's Xander-centric episodes are generally light relief, usually hormone-related. In 'Teacher's Pet', he gets a crush on a biology teacher who turns out to be a preying she-mantis who strings him up in her cellar; in 'Inca Mummy Girl', his essence is nearly drained by a South American mummy posing as an exchange student; in 'Bewitched, Bothered and Bewildered', a love spell backfires and he finds himself pursued by all the women in Sunnydale except the original target of the spell, Cordelia. Xander's dating record is so disastrous, in fact, that by Season Seven, when he meets a nice girl, we can skip directly from their cosy *tête à tête* in a coffee-shop to the inevitable outcome of semi-naked Xander strung up awaiting sacrifice in a basement without need for any of the intermediary steps or exposition. When Dracula sets up shop in Sunnydale in 'Buffy vs Dracula', it's Xander who fills the bug-eating Renfield role, after which he complains, 'I'm sick of being the guy who eats insects and gets the funny syphilis. I'm finished being everybody's butt monkey.'

Of particular note is 'The Zeppo', a variation on the *Rosencrantz and Guildenstern Are Dead* idea of the Big Picture as seen through the eyes of a supporting character. (*Star Trek: The Next Generation* did something similar with an episode called 'The Lower Decks' in which we see the regular cast through the eyes of characters who would normally be no more than walk-on extras.) Xander, who has been relegated to fetching doughnuts for the other Scoobies, narrowly avoids becoming a member of a gang of zombies, loses his virginity to rogue Slayer Faith and saves the school from being blown up, all incidents that go unremarked by the other Scoobies, who are too busy saving the world in a life-or-death crisis which we and Xander can only guess at. ('This is worse than anything we've ever faced,' he overhears Angel saying to Buffy.) While Buffy and Willow are wrestling with the big emotional crises, it's the hunky guy, who in most other TV series would have been cast as the hero, who's assigned the daffy sidekick role traditionally (as in *Doctor Who* or *Adam Adamant*) filled by female characters. Which makes it all the more devastating in Season Six, when he gets cold feet about his marriage to Anya and ditches her at the altar – Xander-centric events that, for once, are not played for laughs.

In Season One, Buffy jokes, 'Let's face it – none of us are ever going to have a happy, normal relationship,' to which Xander replies, 'We're doomed,' and the scene fades out to nervous laughter from the two of them and Willow. It's a prophetic exchange. Relationships in this series are anything but rose-coloured. Even by soap-opera standards, these are *liaisons dangereuses*, and although bad choices can lead not just to heartache but to death, it's the emotional toll that's the heaviest. From Season Two onwards, Buffy is tested by problems that are not so much physical as psychological. 'It turns out to be a question more and more as we work on the series of putting her in peril emotionally,' said Whedon. 'Because she can defeat something doesn't mean that it can't affect her.'[21]

The identity of Season Two's Big Bad is not immediately apparent. At first, it looks set to be (yawn) the Anointed One, an annoying infant leftover from the Master's Season One entourage, but in 'School Hard', the third episode, he's abruptly flash-fried by Spike,whose London accent, black leather coat, black nail varnish, bleached blond hair (he claims Billy Idol stole his look) and an irreverent attitude that immediately sets him apart, even in the generally anarchic world of the undead, and in particular distinguishes

Spike and Dru, the groovy English vampire couple

him from the Master, an old-style villain given to pompous
declamation and ordering minions around. Spike refuses to kowtow to
other vampires who set themselves up as his superiors, despises ritual
and tradition and never loses an opportunity to puncture someone's
balloon. 'If every vampire who said he was at the Crucifixion was
actually there,' he sneers at one such claimant, 'it would have been like
Woodstock.' He and Dru are the ultimate killer couple on the run in
the tradition of film noir (*Gun Crazy* [1950], *They Live by Night*
[1948]) and its more modern variations (*Bonnie and Clyde* [1967], *Sid
and Nancy* [1986], *Natural Born Killers* [1994]). And, unlike the
Master, they know how to enjoy themselves; they throw parties.
Whedon says

the idea of Spike and Dru was to get somebody a little younger, a little bit funkier, who could walk in the lives of our characters and affect them on a romantic level, on a more visceral level than just 'Ooh, I wish I could kill Buffy!', and to bring some real twisted romance to their relationship. [It was] a fun new place to go, it said vampires were even more complex than we thought they were.[22]

Spike and Dru are the first vampire characters whose hopes and dreams extend beyond merely wanting to bite necks and bring about the End of the World, though they're obviously not above that as well.

It isn't until Season Five and the flashbacks in 'Fool for Love' that we find out that Spike is not a natural-born punk. He used to be a nerd. As a human in Victorian London, he was a poet so cringe-makingly bad he made William McGonagall sound like John Keats. (Sample doggerel: 'My heart expands, 'Tis grown a bulge in it, Inspired by your beauty, Effulgent.') He is mocked by his peers, despised by the woman he loves ('You're beneath me') and, as we learn, two seasons later in 'Lies My Parents Told Me', had an unhealthily close relationship with his mother. It's only after Drusilla turns him into a vampire that he's able to give vent to his anarchic rage and lash out at the society that mocked him.

But despite appearances, the Big Bad in Season Two is neither Spike nor Dru. It's not until more than halfway through the season, in 'Innocence', that Whedon drops his bombshell and reveals that it's Angel – or, to be precise, *Angelus*, which is what Angel becomes after he achieves that moment of perfect happiness with Buffy. 'What we basically wanted to show', says Whedon, 'was a horror movie version of the idea, "I sleep with my boyfriend and now he doesn't call me . . . and also he's killing hookers in alleys." '[23]

In horror movies, of course, characters have traditionally been punished for having sex. It's a recurring motif in slasher movies, in which the survivor is the one who has *not* had her jollies. Though this cliché has its roots in Hollywood post-Hays Puritanism (sex is bad, and

57

bad must be punished) it also provides an escape route for lazy screenwriters who can't think of anything better for teenage characters to do prior to being slaughtered, and absolves them of the need to write meaningful dialogue. After all, what teenage audience is going to miss the lack of repartee when they're being distracted by rumpy-pumpy action and the promise of violent retribution at any second? On the other hand, I'm sometimes thankful that the teenage characters in horror movies are so underwritten and obnoxious; imagine how upsetting it would be if we had to watch realistic and likeable young people being sliced and diced willy-nilly.

Whedon himself was torn. 'I said I didn't want to kill the girl who has sex,' he says, 'and yet I punish the shit out of her. That brings up a lot of issues with me.'[24] The scene in which Angelus, still pretending to be Angel, taunts Buffy the morning after consummating their relationship, is particularly harrowing. 'It's a painful scene to watch,' admits Whedon, 'and possibly the best one we've ever done.'[25]

58

Angel: 'Like I really wanted to stick around after *that*?'

Buffy (visibly upset): 'What?'

Angel: 'You've got a lot to learn about men, kiddo, although I guess you proved that last night.'

Buffy is unable to believe her ears. And then Angelus delivers the classic *coup de grâce*: 'I'll call you.'

For the rest of Season Two, Buffy is forced to come to terms with the fact that the man she loved has changed from a sensitive, caring lover into a cruel, cynical heel (not to mention bloodthirsty vampire, but that's by the by). We've all been there, which is why the scene – and the rest of the season with it – packs such a wallop. 'The important thing is to make the punishment emotional,' says Whedon, 'and not have her be axe-murdered, and also let her grow from it, let her grow stronger.'[26] And Buffy does indeed grow stronger, so that she's finally able to sacrifice her boyfriend for the greater good. This being *Buffy the*

Vampire Slayer, however, he's not gone for long. But how can we forgive him after what he's done?

Whedon had already introduced an escape clause in Giles's explanation that a vampire is a demon squatting in a human corpse: 'A vampire isn't a person at all. It may have the movements, the memories, even the personality of the person it takes over, but it is a demon at the core.' Thus, in Season Three, Angel will return from a hell dimension and be rehabilitated as a sympathetic character distinct from the actions of his evil alter ego. It wasn't *his* fault that he killed people, you see – it was the evil demon squatting inside him. It's the supernatural equivalent of schizophrenia, in which someone who's mentally ill would not be held responsible for their actions. But, even with his soul restored, good Angel is acutely aware of the atrocities committed by evil Angelus, so he can continue to be tormented by the memories while seeking redemption. Best of both worlds, for dramatic purposes, and an indicator that not even evil bloodsucking demons are beyond hope.

For most fans, Angel turning evil was the point at which the series really took flight. A previously sympathetic character was going around killing people – including series regular Jenny Calendar, whose corpse he leaves on Giles's bed. 'We learned early on, the scariest thing on the show was people behaving badly, or in peril, morally speaking, or just people getting weird on you – which, by the way, is the scariest thing in life.'[27] But Angel-turning-bad was also a handy solution to a perennial problem: there's nothing more boring in a TV series than a stable relationship (just as in real life there's nothing more tiresome than being trapped in the company of canoodling lovers) and it's the writer's task to find interesting new ways to disrupt that harmony. Whedon calls it 'The Sam and Diane Problem', referring to two main characters in the sitcom *Cheers* (1983–93), but he might just as easily have called it 'The Niles and Daphne' problem (*Frasier*, 1994–) or 'The Ross and Rachel Problem' (*Friends*, 1994–2004) or 'The Maddie and David Problem' (*Moonlighting*, 1985). There's no drama without conflict, and it's a long-standing convention of romances, from the comedies of Shakespeare to *Pride and Prejudice* to Alessandro Manzoni's novel

I Promossi Sposi to *Gone with the Wind* (1939) to *Sleepless in Seattle* (1993), that lovers are kept apart as long as possible. As long as the relationship remains unconsummated, it's titillating and full of potential, though in Buffy's case it's the consummation itself that provides the greatest obstacle to bliss *à deux*. The effect on the relationship of this fundamental difficulty is carried over into Season Three, even after Angel gets his soul back. Once it's established that he and Buffy cannot have sex without him turning evil, the liaison is doomed. They can have – and indeed do have – tender moments of intimacy. They even sleep together, but we are acutely aware that they're never going to get married, or have kids, or live happily ever after, because Angel carries the equivalent of a deadly venereal disease. Of course, one could argue that just because they can't have sexual intercourse doesn't mean he can't fulfil her physical needs while avoiding penetration and ejaculation, but that would open up a whole new can of worms. Could Buffy give him hand relief, for example? Where would that figure on a True Happiness scale of one to ten? In fact, the nearest they get to sex in Season Three is when Faith poisons Angel and, the only antidote being a Slayer's blood, Buffy offers him her neck to suck from. Whedon films the ensuing scene like a love scene, as indeed it is. Fangs piercing flesh is another kind of penetration entirely, of course, but one is still left wondering whether vampires get more of a kick from sucking blood than from regular sexual intercourse and, if so, why wouldn't *that* have provided him with a moment of True Happiness?

In the course of the series, Buffy has several flirtations and three major romantic entanglements (and a single one-night stand), but though her boyfriends are an important part of her life, they're not *all* of her life, and though she often wonders out loud about why she can't keep a man (and quite frankly her record's no worse than mine, and you don't hear me complaining), she can't afford to stay at home, brooding about it; she has a job to do. Buffy is a modern career woman with interests, concerns and responsibilities beyond the remit of a normal couple,

60

though unfortunately for her, it's not a career that pays. ('You can't charge innocent people for saving their lives,' says Dawn in Season Six.) Byron's observation, 'Man's love is of man's life a thing apart, 'Tis woman's whole existence,' holds true only as long as woman has nothing but affairs of the heart to distract her.

Not only does Buffy's calling as the Slayer take precedence over her emotional life, it also gives her preternatural physical and (in time) mental strength, and if the guys can't keep up (as Riley obviously can't in Season Five) then tough. It's only natural she should gravitate towards men whose physical prowess matches her own; in her line of work, this means demons, and it's significant that two of her three entanglements are with vampires, who are at least physically more compatible than most of the other demons she encounters, though it's a shame she never fell for a bloke with horns or scaly skin – something that would have *really* challenged the Californian body aesthetic.

But the underlying message is clear: Buffy can't rely on her boyfriends to help her fulfil her destiny; they *do* lend a hand from time to time, but the bottom line is she's on her own. There isn't any prince who's going to ride up on a white horse and rescue her, just as he rescued Snow White or Sleeping Beauty, because in the Buffyverse, Buffy is both princess *and* prince.

61

5 The Dark Side

What Happens in Season Three

After a brief identity crisis and a stint working as a waitress in another town, Buffy returns to Sunnydale an older, wiser and altogether sadder Slayer. Joyce is still having problems adjusting to her daughter's slaying activities, but Giles forces Principal Snyder to readmit Buffy to Sunnydale High. A naked and traumatised Angel is spat out by the hell dimension where he has been subjected to untold centuries of torment; Buffy tends to him in secret (and gives him something to wear) and, after rehabilitation and a great deal of recrimination and suspicion on the part of everyone except the Slayer, he finally resumes his role fighting alongside the Scoobies. And the death of Kendra at the end of Season Two has 'activated' a new Slayer: Faith, a sexy and impetuous trailer-trash minx who seems to enjoy slaying just a little too much. For a while, it looks as though she's going to be a bad influence on Buffy.

On Buffy's eighteenth birthday, representatives from the Watchers' Council arrive from England to subject her to a dangerous test in which she is drugged (without her knowledge) and pitted against a mad vampire; she passes with flying colours, but her already tenuous respect for the Council and its traditions is weakened even further when Giles is fired for having been too fatherly towards his charge. Wesley Wyndham-Pryce, an Englishman even stuffier than Giles, arrives in

Sunnydale to take over as Buffy's Watcher, but she and her friends find it hard to take him seriously and continue to look to Giles for advice and phlebotinin.

Xander and Willow guiltily embark on a secret kissing relationship, but are caught in flagrante by Cordelia and Oz. Willow and Oz eventually get back together, but Xander and Cordy are history. Anyanka, a vengeance demon, grants Cordy's wish that Buffy had never come to Sunnydale and creates an alternative, vampire-ridden Buffyverse, but Giles destroys Anyanka's amulet, reversing the spell and trapping Anyanka in the human body of Anya, a high-school student. Cordelia and Wesley are mutually attracted, but the attraction fails to survive their first kiss (which is probably just as well-since she's a student and he's virtually a teacher).

Demons-of-the-week include zombie party-crashers, an evil Watcher, a demon assuming the form of murdered children to dupe Sunnydale parents (led by Joyce and Willow's mom) into trying to burn their daughters at the stake, and a candy bar that makes all the adults in Sunnydale behave like irresponsible teenagers; while under the influence, Joyce and Giles have sex (twice) on the bonnet of a police car. The new Big Bad is Richard Wilkins III, Mayor of Sunnydale, a genial but thoroughly evil figure who is preparing for his 'Ascension', when he will assume demonic form. Faith accidentally kills a human, the Deputy Mayor, and tries to pin the blame on Buffy. Increasingly isolated and alienated from the Scoobies, Faith finally crosses to the Dark Side and joins the Mayor, with whom she bonds in a strong (but evil) father–daughter relationship.

Angel becomes acutely aware that his relationship with Buffy will prevent her from leading a 'normal' life; Buffy is heartbroken when he tells her of his intention to leave town after Graduation Day. Faith shoots him with a poisoned crossbow bolt, but is left in a coma after a pitched battle against Buffy. Buffy lets Angel drink her blood to restore him to rude vampire health just in time for Graduation Day, when the Mayor morphs into a giant snake demon which eats Principal Snyder, but Buffy and the Scoobies organise the rest of the students into fighting back against his vampire minions. Many are killed in the struggle (including Harmony, one of Cordy's former clique, who's bitten by a vampire), but Buffy finally destroys the demon by blowing up the school.

Angel leaves Sunnydale for Los Angeles, where he will become the hero of his own series, *Angel*. Cordelia heads for Hollywood to become a movie star, but will end up joining Angel in his fight against evil, as will, eventually, Wesley Wyndham-Pryce.

Sunnydale is 'two hours on the freeway from Neiman Marcus', which by my calculations (the Californian speed limit on freeways being a stately seventy mph) makes it 140 miles from Beverly Hills. Los Angeles, as we all know, has long been regarded as the centre of the known universe in films and TV shows, largely because most of them are shot there; aliens or giant meteors can obliterate Europe or Asia with impunity, but it's only when the United States, and Los Angeles in particular, are menaced that the threat is taken seriously. Thus Sunnydale is near enough to Los Angeles to make it a sort of annex, in which LA mores, speech patterns and all-round idiocy hold sway, yet sufficiently remote to grant it demonic autonomy. Strangely (you would have thought all that demonic activity would have made good copy), the media are not a big deal in Sunnydale; reporters and TV crews do not descend in droves on every new manifestation of the uncanny, and TV reporting of town-wide phenomena (such as the communal loss of voice in 'Hush', ascribed to widespread laryngitis) is the exception rather than the rule.

At first sight, Sunnydale seems to be a typical Californian town, of the type seen so often on TV and in films – a setting for sitcoms, teen dramas or soap operas, more an American state of mind than a realistic location. Everyone – even supposedly less privileged characters such as Xander – looks sleek and healthy, no-one (excepting certain demons) has bad skin or wears the same outfit two episodes running. The students are predominantly Caucasian and many of them, including Cordelia, have cars. (Unusually for a supernaturally themed TV show,

64

Buffy will find herself faced with realistic financial problems, but that's not until Season Six.)

Sunnydale, as its name and the West Coast location imply, is sufficiently sunny to make bad weather seem strange and unnatural. The arrival of Dracula as a guest star in Season Five is heralded by a violent rainstorm, while in Season Three there's even a snowstorm, but otherwise, in best Californian style, the seasons blend into one. Halloween, Christmas, Buffy's birthday pass by every year with no marked changes in temperature or the characters' wardrobes. For the girls, micro-mini skirts and skimpy camisole tops are invariably the order of the day.

Vampires, demons, witches, werewolves – all this supernatural activity in a single place might pass unremarked in a big city like New York or Los Angeles, but the rationalisation for this superabundance of unpleasantness in a single small town is Sunnydale's location on 'The Hellmouth', a sort of paranormal San Andreas fault that acts like a homing device in attracting demonic entities from all parts of the globe, as well as threatening to disgorge further horrors at any moment. In Whedon's words, the Hellmouth is 'a shortcut, in lieu of scientific explanation'.[28] (Inspector Morse could have done with a similar pretext to explain the preternaturally high murder rate in sleepy Oxford.) It's a topological MacGuffin that basically gives the writers carte blanche to make of Sunnydale what they will.

Sunnydale has everything, and more, that the inhabitants of a small town could possibly desire, except perhaps supermarkets, of which there seems to be a shortage. The fridge in Buffy's house is invariably well stocked, but we never see anyone shopping for food, though they do occasionally phone out for pizza. But there is a shopping mall, and a club-cum-coffee-bar called the Bronze, where the students congregate after hours to drink coffee, listen to music, dance and – occasionally – drink alcohol. (Although the series' background music is principally lush and orchestral, the Bronze provides a weekly showcase for pop and rock bands such as Cibo Matto, or The Breeders.) When Cordelia first tells Buffy about the Bronze, she says, 'It's in the bad part of town', and when Buffy asks where that is, says, 'about half a block from the good part of town. We don't have a whole lot of town.'

Nevertheless, as the series progresses, Sunnydale's city limits expand miraculously to encompass whatever locations may be required for story purposes. There are twelve cemeteries where Buffy can stake newly risen vampires (though it's assumed she is always patrolling the same one) and forty-three churches, which is perhaps excessive by smalltown standards, though none of the regular characters are churchgoers (Willow is non-practising Jewish). There's a main street, occasionally thronged by extras, and a disproportionate number of garbage-strewn alleyways for vampires to lurk in. There's a funeral parlour, scene of many a corpse revival, and a magic shop which increases in importance when Giles buys it in Season Five, when it takes over from the school library and Giles's own apartment as Scooby HQ.

There are docks and a beach, bus and railway stations and an airport (though travellers must go to LAX for international flights), a cinema and an ice-rink, a choice of restaurants including a burger joint called the Doublemeat Palace, where Buffy goes to work in Season Six, and a romantic candle-lit French restaurant, where she is wined and dined by Principal Wood in Season Seven. There's a police station, museum, bank, park and zoo, city hall and university, Sunnydale UC, which was built over the remains of an old Mission, buried by an earthquake in 1812. Also beneath the university is a huge underground military complex which no-one notices until Season Four. There's a convent, where Buffy saves a nun from a vampire, and a nearby army base, where Xander steals a rocket-launcher, and Willie's Bar, where the demons hang out. There are numerous old factories and decrepit warehouses and abandoned mansions and, in 'Buffy vs Dracula', a castle. (Riley: 'I've lived in Sunnydale a couple of years now, and what I've never noticed before . . .' Giles: 'Er, a castle?') Like the show itself, the town expands or contracts to fit the writers' demands. Anything goes, just as long as they can come up with a workable supernatural pretext.

There are also streets full of civilian dwellings fronted by well-tended lawns. Buffy lives at number 1630 Revello Drive (which suggests a road in a big city rather than smalltown proportions). On the surface, Sunnydale is the very model of the sort of small town that in film after film (*Doc Hollywood* [1991], *Groundhog Day* [1993], *Runaway Bride* [1999], *Mr Deeds* [2002], *Sweet Home Alabama* [2002] *et al.*) is held up as a safe, wholesome alternative to urban sprawls such as Los Angeles, New York, San Francisco or Miami. American TV crime series, unlike their British counterparts, are set less frequently in small towns than in big cities, traditionally depicted as hotbeds of corruption, pollution, drugs, prostitution and an inexhaustible stream of murders to solve. Big American cities, moreover, are seen as melting pots of immigrants from older cultures. Architecture and commerce are based on models drawn from Old Europe, whereas the genuine untainted America is supposedly embodied in the smalltown values of green fields, picket fences, happy families and cheery neighbours – the sort of image so patently artificial it's practically a parody of postwar consumerism and the idealised American family life of *Leave It to Beaver* or *The Andy Griffith Show* (for which, may I remind you, Whedon's grandfather wrote), spoofed so mercilessly in *The Simpsons* (1989–).

67

I can't be the only European visitor to feel more at home in America's big coastal conurbations than in any of the places in between, the 'red' Republican-voting states, the so-called Heartland and the Midwest, Mississippi, Dust Bowl and the Rockies, which we picture as a vast wilderness criss-crossed by deserted highways, patrolled by psychopathic cops and scattered with hick towns and truckstops populated by chainsaw-wielding maniacs, crazed hillbillies, alien pod-people, book-burners, racists, religious maniacs and Norman Bates. A ridiculous generalisation, it's true, but a perception shared, I suspect, by many Europeans of my generation whose view of non-urban America has essentially been coloured by our exposure to towns like Strand (*Fury*, 1948), Black Rock (*Bad Day at Black Rock*, 1954), Santa Mira (*Invasion of the Body Snatchers*, 1956), Peyton Place, Climax (*Kiss Me, Stupid*, 1964), Lumberton (*Blue Velvet*, 1986), Twin Peaks, Salem's Lot, Castle Rock and, *in extremis*, the hostile boondocks of *Deliverance* (1972) and *The Texas Chainsaw Massacre* (1974), where the locals are inbred and the sheriff is in league with the psychos. David Lynch said: 'I like the idea that everything has a surface which hides much more underneath. Someone can look very well and have a whole bunch of diseases cooking: there are all sorts of dark, twisted things lurking down there.'[29] And since smalltown America is supposed to embody the cornfed values of real America, it follows that the diseases lurking beneath it are the diseases afflicting America itself – malaises normally kept under wraps, such as repression, hypocrisy, lust, greed, adultery, intolerance, cruelty, not to mention fiendish amounts of bloodsucking and demon worship.

Of course, Sunnydale's dark underbelly isn't just metaphorical; beneath the town (and presumably just above the Hellmouth) lies a warren of sewers, caverns and tunnels, a warped reflection of the above-ground Sunnydale, enabling communities of vampires and other monsters to exist in a grotesque parody of the real town. The caves and tunnels provide not just lairs for the vampires, but a means by which they can travel across town without being exposed to sunlight. (The other way for vampires to get around during daylight hours, as frequently demonstrated by Angel and Spike, is running very fast with head and shoulders shielded by a smouldering blanket.)

The naming of towns in American popular culture is often on the nail (Smallville, Eerie, Mystery, Bedrock, Gotham City) or an excuse for a pun (Arcadia as in *Joan of Arcadia* (2003–5), Neptune as in *Veronica Mars* [2004–]) or ironic (Perfection, Amityville, Trinity, Point Pleasant). While its West Coast location is a virtual guarantee of good weather, Sunnydale falls into the ironic category, though if its founders had wanted to be more on the nail they should have called it Hellmouth (which, for British viewers, conjures up visions of an overheated seaside resort). We're told that the Spanish colonial name for Sunnydale was Boca del Infierno, which suggests the Hellmouth has been around even longer than the town. What manner of horror might it have unleashed before the coming of Europeans? The coyote and lizard demons of Native American mythology? Relatives of the Inca Mummy Girl from Season Two? Or does the Hellmouth owe its very existence to the arrival of Europeans, who decimated the native populations with Old World scourges such as smallpox, measles and vampires? Most of the monsters are not homegrown, but find their way into town via the portals of the museum, art gallery, zoo or docks. With the exception of Darla (a prostitute sired by the Master in a seventeenth-century Virginia colony), all the oldest and most evil vampires and demons in the series hail from Old Europe. They are not just illegal immigrants without Green Cards, they are corruptors of the New World, like escapees from some psychopathic Henry James novel aiming to besmirch American innocence – ironic considering that nowadays it's Old World youth that's more often thought of as being in danger of corruption by the pervasive fast food and pop culture of America.

Sunnydale was founded in 1899 by Richard Wilkins III, the Big Bad of Season Three. He has been the Mayor for a hundred years, though since he has spent the last century paying tribute to various demons in return for long life and power, he doesn't look a day over fifty. Ominous hints are dropped about him throughout Season Two, so by the time we finally get to meet him in the flesh, it's a shock to find he's not the sinister-looking villain we've been expecting, but a pious, golly-gee-shucks all-American guy. In his office in City Hall is a cabinet containing not bottles of alcohol, but ancient relics, skulls, orbs – and a box of tissues, for the Mayor has a Howard Hughes-like phobia about germs ('My dear mother said cleanliness was next to Godliness'). He's *Buffy the Vampire Slayer*'s most effective villain because he represents more than just a desire to kill Buffy or save the world – like Judge Axel, Reaganite head of the vampire community in Larry Cohen's 1987 horror satire *A Return to Salem's Lot* (which apart from its title has little to do with King's novel), Wilkins is a figurehead of civic power, politics, public office, as efficient as he is corrupt. All the signs are that, aside from his evil ambitions, he is a pretty good mayor who takes his duties seriously (his list of Things To Do includes: Greet scouts, Plumber union reschedule, Call temp agency, Become invincible, Meeting with PTA, Haircut). He's all the more frightening because he looks so normal,

69

though his Ascension will ultimately transform him, in possibly the series' shoddiest special effect, into a giant snake demon. He's the sort of fellow who, just after he's survived having been chopped in half (being invincible will do that), will chirp, 'Gosh, I'm feeling chipper. Who's for a root beer?' You could just see him in the White House.

Just as Sunnydale has its dark side, so do our heroes. As Spider-Man learns, 'With great power comes great responsibility', and in Season Three we see what happens when that power is abused. Buffy's evil id is incarnated by the rogue Slayer, Faith. Whedon explains,

> 'Bad Girls' and 'Consequences' were our attempt to start exploring the
> idea of being a Slayer in terms of the power of it . . . Because we didn't

Mayor Richard Wilkins III: 'Well, gosh . . .'

want to send Buffy into too dark a place where we didn't like her any
more, we used Faith's character as the person who might . . . take it too
far.[30]

Where Buffy is blonde and perky, Faith is a smouldering brunette. Buffy
wears white or pink or powder-blue girly ensembles; Faith wears punky
black, with lots of leather and cleavage. She's aggressive and sexy,
adorned by tattoos, dark lipstick and kohl, a 'Riot Grrrl' who laughs in
the face of danger and makes Buffy look prissy, spoilt and cautious by
comparison. Faith grew up in a trailer, and lacks the network of family
and friends that keeps Buffy grounded. She's upfront about getting an
erotic thrill out of slaying, which she treats as some kind of extreme
sport. She's Buffy's dark twin, though the writers are too savvy to make
her out-and-out malevolent; her tough exterior conceals deep
psychological scars, and it's her lack of emotional support – and refusal
to admit to it – that makes her vulnerable and, ultimately, ripe for
redemption.

At first she and Buffy make a great tag-staking team, until
finally, in 'Bad Girls', her malign influence on Buffy begins to show.
There's a new Watcher in town, the effete Wesley Wyndham-Pryce, so
repressed and prissy he makes Giles look rebellious. Buffy thinks he's 'a
dork', but is nevertheless prepared to take orders from him. 'What else
can we do?' she asks Faith, who replies, 'Whatever we want. We're
Slayers, girlfriend, the Chosen Two.' And for a while, at least, Buffy
believes her. She plays truant from class and joins Faith on the dance
floor of the Bronze in some sexy frugging that has all the jocks (and
presumably all the male adolescent viewers as well) panting with desire.
She and Faith are arrested for breaking into a store in search of weapons
(Faith's motto is 'Want, take, have'), but escape from police custody,
treating the escapade as a grand lark. But this naughty girl behaviour
goes horribly wrong during a gung-ho vampire slaying when Faith
mistakenly plunges a stake into the heart of a human being. Buffy is
horrified, but Faith pretends not to care. 'We're warriors, we're built to
kill,' she says. 'To kill *demons*,' protests Buffy. 'It does not mean that we

71

The Chosen Two: Faith and Buffy on the dance floor

get to pass judgement, that we're better than everyone else.' Faith, however, insists, 'We *are* better.'

Faith not only refuses to take responsibility for her actions, but tries to lay the blame on Buffy and finds herself alienated from the Scoobies as a consequence. 'In different circumstances that could be me,' says Buffy, spelling it out. When Faith turns up on the Mayor's doorstep, offering her services, he is delighted to find himself with a Slayer sidekick and surrogate daughter. He showers her with gifts – a pretty frock, swanky new apartment and a wicked-looking Rambo knife – and, starved of a father figure, she responds by turning into his cold-blooded hitwoman. Just prior to the season finale, Buffy and Faith engage in a knock-down, no-holds-barred catfight which ends with Faith in a coma.

Mayor Wilkins loses his cool for the very first time and incidentally provides Buffy with the means to exploit his only weakness in the final showdown. Whereas emotional ties make Buffy and the good guys stronger, for the bad guys they're an Achilles' heel. The snake demon's last words, before he's blown to kingdom come, are 'Well gosh . . .'

Season Three is all about dark sides, and an episode called 'The Wish' shows what would have happened if the surface of Sunnydale had ever come to resemble its underbelly. It's the Buffyverse version of *It's a Wonderful Life* (1946) and an example of that favourite science-fiction standby – the alternative universe, exemplified in the *Star Trek* episode 'Mirror, Mirror', in which the Federation is not the benign futuristic intergalactic version of the UN, but an evil empire. An entire TV series, *Sliders* (1995–2000), was dedicated to the premise of a handful of people travelling through alternative versions of San Francisco in an attempt to get back to their own. It's a mainstay of speculative fiction as well, in novels such as Keith Roberts' *Pavane* (Queen Elizabeth I was assassinated), Kingsley Amis' *The Alteration* (the Reformation never took place), Philip K. Dick's *Man in the High Castle* (the Axis powers won World War II), Robert Harris' *Fatherland* (Nazi Germany was victorious), while Ray Bradbury's short story 'A Sound of Thunder' (brilliantly parodied in *The Simpsons*' 'Time and Punishment') demonstrates how a seemingly insignificant event (the squashing of a butterfly in the Jurassic era) can alter the world millions of years later.

The butterfly-squashing pivotal moment of 'The Wish' is Cordelia wishing Buffy Summers had never come to Sunnydale, unaware she's doing it in the presence of a vengeance demon with the power to make the wish come true. The episode deepens rather than advances the story arc by emphasising the show's mission statement, announced in the opening teaser in which Xander and Willow (rather clumsily) help Buffy kill a demon and she responds with an over-generous, 'If you guys hadn't been here to help . . .'

Alternative universes invariably paint a darker picture, as opposed to a world in which all the imperfections have been ironed out.

73

Alternative universes resembling Gardens of Eden tend to harbour serpents. As Professor Farnsworth puts it in 'The Farnsworth Parabox', a parallel universe episode of *Futurama*, 'When you create a parallel universe, it's almost always populated by evil twins.' 'The Wish' adheres to this convention by making the alternative Sunnydale worse than regular Sunnydale, Hellmouth and all. If Buffy had never come to Sunnydale, there would have been no-one to defeat the Master who, despite token resistance from Giles, Oz and a few others, is poised to take over the town. He and his vampires have established their HQ in the Bronze, where they're preparing to launch their 'Final Solution' – an automated plant to extract blood through tubes injected into a still-living human victim. Xander and Willow are no longer geeks; death has turned

The Dark Side: Willow and Xander as vampires in the alternative Sunnydale of 'The Wish'

them into vampires, dressed to kill in black leather and, in Willow's case, a sexy corset top. They get their kicks from hunting and biting humans, or from torturing Angel, who's chained up in a cell for their amusement. The streets of Sunnydale echo with the sound of distant screams. The shops are shuttered. There's a curfew and – seemingly a habitual characteristic in the breakdown of civilisation – lots of litter.

This is not the Sunnydale that we know. It throws us off balance, and for something that starts off as a light-hearted premise, this is a dark, dark vision, not a town we would want to linger in for more than an episode. Cordy realises her error, and just has time to say to Giles, 'You have to get Buffy. Buffy changes it. It wasn't like this – it was better, the clothes alone,' before she's killed by Xander and her corpse is cast into a furnace. And with her goes our last link to the 'real' world; we're left stranded in alternative Sunnydale, without a guide.

Prompted by Cordy's talk of Buffy, Giles gets on the phone and learns the Slayer has been too busy fighting demons in Cleveland to come to Sunnydale. When she finally arrives, just in time to save Giles from a vampire attack, it's immediately apparent this is a very different Slayer from the one we know and love. She's dressed not in pretty clothes but in workmanlike singlet and fatigue pants. She's a no-nonsense, hard-bitten, battle-scarred and cynical warrior, with not a trace of the Barbie doll cheerleader. This, more than anything, points up the difference between Buffy and her forebears – Ripley from the *Alien* films, and the pumped-up Sarah Connor from *Terminator 2: Judgment Day*. If the *Alien* tetralogy is 'about' anything, other than the obvious fight against the creatures, it's about what it means to be human. After four films of ducking and weaving and fighting, is it enough for Ripley merely to survive? At what point does the struggle for survival turn a person into an automaton? As Sigourney Weaver said of the character she played in *Alien* and its sequels, 'This is about the quality of life. At what point do you say existence per se is not worth it? What is it that makes life worth living and fighting for?'[31]

It's a question that is continually, albeit for the most part implicitly, addressed throughout the seven seasons of *Buffy the Vampire*

Slayer. Like Ripley and Sarah Connor, the alternative Buffy of 'The Wish' has been forced to sacrifice her humanity to become a fighting machine. For her, the struggle for survival has taken over. This is how Buffy would have been if she'd never made friends with Xander, Willow and Giles – still a heroine, but a loner, a Mad Maxine, who waves aside Giles's proposal to investigate Cordelia's wish in favour of direct action. She's happy to go it alone and leave Giles to his mystic dabbling – 'I don't play well with others.' This is a Slayer who has no friends or allies, no time for fun and games, who is used to getting the job done without frills and pretty clothes. 'The world is what it is,' she says. 'We fight and we die.' She arrives at the Bronze and plunges into battle, just as the Master is saying, 'Welcome to the future.' And because this alternative Buffy is a loner, she dies.

She's not the only one to bite the dust. In one last chaotic fight, we see Xander staking Angel. Buffy stakes Xander without even blinking. And why should she blink? In this world, they've never even met. Oz stakes Willow – to him she's just another vampire. And the Master, finally, breaks Buffy's neck, and ...

Fortunately for the future of the series, Giles succeeds in destroying Anyanka's power source and we're whisked back into the real Sunnydale, to where Buffy, Xander, Willow and Giles are all smiling and laughing in the sunshine, unaware that anything out of the ordinary has taken place. Cordy has no memory of it either; the only character aware of what has happened is Anyanka, now condemned to a human existence as Anya, who will shortly start dating Xander and become a series regular. Anya and Xander will spend a lot of time together; one wonders if she ever mentions the events of 'The Wish' to him, the way she mentions other alternative universes in the Scoobies' presence: the World without Shrimp, the Land of the Trolls, the Land of Perpetual Wednesday and Crazy Melty Land. Alas, we don't get to see any of these.

Thus, in 'The Wish', everything is magically resolved in an upbeat ending, but we're left feeling uneasy. We've seen all our characters changed for the worse, and we've seen all of them (except Giles and Oz, and we don't hold out much hope for either of them) die. Death on such a devastating scale is not something you often get to experience in a mid-season episode of an amusing, teen-oriented series set in high school. (Most of the regular characters on *Blake's 7* were killed off, but only in the final episode of the series, while most of the fatalities in *Dynasty*'s infamous Moldavian wedding massacre turn out to have miraculously survived.) We know it was only an alternative universe and that everything is back to normal – or as normal as it ever gets in *Buffy the Vampire Slayer*. But we can't forget what we've seen. The show continues, but the memory lingers on.

Of course, any work of fiction is *already* an alternative universe, a looking-glass world that offers a reflection of our own reality. The 'normal' world of *Star Trek*, for example, is an idealised future. The 'normal' world according to *Sliders* is a reality consisting of parallel universes. The 'normal' world of *Friends* is an idealised depiction of six young adults in an idealised New York City. The Buffyverse is an easily identifiable version of our own real world, populated by characters who think and act in familiar ways, even if some of them just happen to be vampires. The events may be fantastic, but the emotions are not.

'The Wish' is the series' first alternative universe episode, but not the last. 'Superstar' in Season Four reintroduces us to the character of Jonathan Levenson, Sunnydale's perennial fall-guy, victim and a former classmate so nerdy he makes Xander and Willow look cool. Unbeknown to the other characters (and to us, to begin with) he has cast a spell in which he's a James Bond-style superagent, seasoned vampire slayer, sex-god, psychological counsellor, Sinatra-style crooner, jazz musician, tactical consultant to the military, chess grandmaster, bestselling author, inventor of the Internet and star of *The Matrix* – the average nerd's wish fulfilment list, in other words. This time, the episode plunges us right into the alternative universe, without introductory explanation, as the Scoobies defer, without irony, to Jonathan's superiority in vampire hunting, computers and chess. Even the now familiar credits are doctored to include hitherto unseen images of Jonathan in heroic mode, and it's not until halfway through the episode that anyone acknowledges there's anything amiss.

Rather darker is a Season Six episode called 'Normal Again', in which Buffy finds herself an inmate in a mental institution, where the doctors and parents insist that vampire slaying, demons and monsters, her friends and her sister Dawn are all part of an elaborate fantasy world she has conjured up to avoid facing reality. Rather daringly, the episode proposes that all previous six seasons of *Buffy the Vampire Slayer* have been taking place in her head, much as the characters in the 'Back to Reality' episode of *Red Dwarf* (1988) are told that their five seasons of outer space adventures have been nothing more than a virtual-reality computer game they've been playing – and playing badly, at that. The kicker in Buffy's case, though, is that she's going through such a rough time in her real world that she's tempted to surrender to an alternate, more mundane reality in which her mother is still alive, her parents are still together and she no longer has to bear the weight of the world on her shoulders, a reality in which she is, in fact, just an ordinary girl. It's an indication of how well the writers have done their work that we now find ourselves rooting for her not to relinquish six seasons' worth of preposterous events in favour of the easier, non-heroic but more realistic option.

Buffy the Vampire Slayer is a show in which, sooner or later, *everyone* gets to show their darker side. Angel becomes Angelus. Giles becomes Ripper. Willow becomes Dark Willow. Xander meets his own doppelgänger. Oz turns into a werewolf. Spike and Anya start off dark and go into reverse, as it were, though with occasional relapses. Buffy's dark side is not just represented by Faith, but by her own appearance as a manifestation of the First Evil in the final season. Cordelia is presumably so disagreeable as a personality that she doesn't *need* a dark side (or maybe it's just because she's irredeemably shallow), though she makes up for it later when she follows Angel into his own series, where she will ultimately turn evil and give birth to the Anti-Christ. And you can't get more dark-sidey than that.

6 Higher Learning

What Happens in Season Four

Buffy and Willow go to college. Xander sets out to see America, Kerouac-style, but doesn't get far. On his return to Sunnydale he moves into his parents' basement and tries his hand at various jobs, such as ice-cream vendor and construction worker. Giles, who no longer has a library to tend, feels 'out of the loop-y'. Professor Maggie Walsh, Buffy's psychology teacher, turns out to be the head of the Initiative, a government-funded organisation that has set up shop in a vast underground HQ beneath the university, from where it surveys the local paranormal activity and conducts scientific experiments on captured demons.

      Buffy has a one-night stand with a student called Parker before embarking on a more enduring relationship with Riley, a student who turns out to be a member of the Initiative's secret military unit. Spike returns to Sunnydale with his new vampire girlfriend, Harmony; the Initiative plants a chip in his brain that prevents him from biting or otherwise attacking humans. He has no problem beating up demons, however, so ends up fighting alongside the Scoobies, though they still don't trust him, and with good reason. Oz's animal side gets the better of him and he has sex with a female werewolf; dismayed by his own behaviour, he leaves town. Willow is heartbroken, but forms a close bond with a student and fellow wiccan called Tara. When Oz returns, having learnt to control his inner wolf, Willow chooses to stay with Tara; Oz takes off again, this time for good. Faith wakes from her coma and, with the help of a gizmo left by the Mayor, swaps bodies with Buffy; while in Buffy's body, she has sex with Riley but subsequently shows the first inklings of Slayer conscience before Buffy manages to reverse the body swap.

Riley introduces Buffy to the Initiative, but her independent spirit alarms Maggie Walsh, who sends her into a trap. Buffy escapes unharmed, and Walsh is killed by one of her own experiments: a demon–human hybrid called Adam, the season's Big Bad, who is plotting to create an invincible army of demon–human hybrids. Adam promises to remove the chip from Spike's brain in return for the vampire's sowing seeds of discord among the Scoobies, but the friends resolve their differences just in time for the final showdown with the Big Bad's hybrid army in the Initiative HQ, and Spike's chip remains. Buffy finally defeats Adam with help from the other Scoobies, who meld their minds, enabling her to draw on the mystical power of the First Slayer.

What is there left to do after you've blown up your school? With the last shot of Season Three, as the camera finally came to rest on an abandoned copy of the Sunnydale High School Yearbook, I burst into tears, knowing this was as good as it could possibly get. Whatever happened next could only be anti-climax. Whereas in real life I couldn't wait to leave school, now I wanted to stay there for ever, fighting demons in the company of Buffy and her friends; this is what my schooldays *should* have been like.

But now, along with the writers, I was forced to leave the familiar high-school genre behind. What can you do with a high-school horror comedy when your characters are no longer in high school? Leaving school is a big leap into the unknown, one of the biggest upheavals in life, let alone in a TV series; Season Four reflects this uncertainty, groping around for a new format to replace the old. 'We pretty much played out high school . . .' says Whedon, 'and yet college is very much the same and also completely different, in the freedom you get and the incredible stupidity it causes.'[32]

As the Slayer, Buffy accepts she has no choice but to stay near the Hellmouth, so she enrols at Sunnydale UC as opposed to, say, Yale or the Shaolin School for Slayers. But whereas swotty Willow seems to slot right in at university, Buffy finds herself back at square one – unsure of herself and her new situation, though her role will unquestionably involve vampire slaying, as the season's first episode demonstrates. The first new friend she makes is promptly vampirised by a fanged campus clique whose leader makes fun of Buffy's lack of college nous. Her disorientation mirrors our own; we wish we were back at Sunnydale High! Vampires or no vampires, we knew where we were with school, who everyone was and how things worked. But now we're being forced, if not into the wide world, then at least into a more grown-up environment. *But we don't want to grow up!*

Even worse than the disorientation, for the viewer, is the sense of something missing, and we're not just talking Angel and Cordelia, who've gone off to LA. From Season Four onwards, Joss Whedon would be dividing his energy between *Buffy the Vampire Slayer* and its spin-off series, *Angel*. 'I was literally on set for three years on *Buffy*. And then all of a sudden I couldn't be on . . . set that much.'[33] As late as Season Four, however, writer Jane Espenson claims, 'There's not a line that he has not approved and there's not a story that has not largely been, not just influenced by him, but really pitched by him.'[34]

Whedon is to the Buffyverse what the character of Christof was to *The Truman Show* (1998) – nothing less than the Creator – and the episodes he writes and directs in the last four seasons seem increasingly like the experiments of a capricious deity toying with his characters, playing with format and genre, or gleefully ripping holes in the fourth wall between the show and its audience. In 'Hush', he deprives his characters of speech. In 'Restless', he exposes their dreams to our gaze. In 'The Body', he kills off a regular character and coolly observes the others' reactions to real as opposed to supernatural death. And in 'Once More, with Feeling', he sadistically forces them to sing and

81

dance. This is some of the most audacious and original material ever to make it on to a popular prime-time show and each of these episodes is a corker, but they're formal experiments in a one-off forty-minute format, rather than the development of a continuing series in new and unexpected directions.

Though Whedon wrote and directed four episodes in Season Four, there is a discernible decline not so much in the quality of the show – the dialogue is as witty as ever – as in the overall cohesion. For the first time, my TV attention-deficit disorder began to kick in and I sometimes found my thoughts wandering, something which would have been unthinkable during the first three seasons. The biggest problem, never quite overcome, is the switch from high-school to college setting. In 1999, when Season Four was first aired, the college genre was a lot less clearly defined than its high-school equivalent and seemed mostly to revolve around male students getting drunk and trying to get laid. College movies hadn't been taken seriously since the early 1970s, when a Hollywood flirtation with campus unrest and counter culture (in films such as *The Strawberry Statement*, *Getting Straight* and *Drive, He Said* [all 1970]) petered out, paving the way for the bad behaviour of *National Lampoon's Animal House* (1978) and *Revenge of the Nerds* (1984). Despite rare 'serious' dramas such as *The Paper Chase* (which in 1978 engendered a TV series that proved to have more staying power than the same year's *Animal House* spin-off, *Delta House*), the John Hughes effect that had bestowed a modicum of respectability on 1980s high-school movies didn't extend into further education. Television, too, fought shy of college, perhaps because most real-life students have better things to do than to watch TV. The gormless, campy *Saved by the Bell* (1989–93) spawned the short-lived *Saved by the Bell: The College Years* (1993–4), set at California University, but when the series was later resurrected it was back to school for *Saved by the Bell: The New Class* (1993–2000). The teens of *Beverly Hills 90210* and *Dawson's Creek* (1998–2004) graduated to college as well, though the shows kept rolling on as though nothing had changed. Films that attempted to take the college experience seriously – such as *Higher Learning* (1995), which tackles racism, sexism and date rape (the victim, incidentally, being played by Kristy Swanson, the original Buffy) – were exceptions, and at the start of the twenty-first century, a new wave of college movies (*American Pie 2* [2001], *Road Trip* [2000], *Van Wilder: Party Liaison* [2002], *Old School* [2003]) was still cleaving to the *Animal House* model and recycling the old male-students-behaving-badly routine. College movies depicting young women as anything other than fantasy sex objects can be counted on the fingers of one hand, and even fewer placed them centre stage, though *The Rules of Attraction* (2002) at least grants equal sex, drug and stupidity opportunities to both genders.

Season Four, like Buffy herself, begins by making a conscientious attempt to live college life to the full. In the early episodes, we see her attending a number of lectures, but of all the tutors and professors, it's only Maggie Walsh who is allowed to develop into a recurring character. Buffy has Single White Female-type problems with her room-mate (who with her food-labelling and clothes-borrowing is impossible to live with, even before she's unmasked as a demon), attends frat-house parties (which invariably turn out to be hexed or haunted) and indulges in such typical student pursuits as one-night stands (Parker, who looks all set to become her post-Angel romantic interest, turns out to be a heel) and drinking beer (which turns students into Cro-Magnon cave people, much as it does in real life). It's business as usual, in other words, with Buffy juggling slaying and college life just as she juggled slaying and school work. But as Season Four progresses, it becomes clear that college and vampire slaying *don't* mix. Buffy's attendance at lectures becomes less frequent until Sunnydale UC ends up shunted aside by the Initiative, and from then on we don't hear much about college until she drops out altogether in Season Five.

83

Other than Willow's new friend Tara, the only students to make their mark are Riley and his buddy Forrest, who both lead secret lives as Initiative soldiers. More damagingly, the build-up to the showdown with the Big Bad is nowhere near as compelling as in past seasons. This is partly because the formula's getting a little threadbare; by now, no fewer than six Ends of the World have been narrowly

averted, a fact acknowledged in 'Doomed', when Giles's warning of yet
another apocalypse is greeted by the Scoobies chorusing, 'Again?' But
it's also because the subplot involving the Initiative never really slots
comfortably into place. It's only logical that the US government and
military would notice the superabundance of paranormal activity in
Sunnydale, but the introduction of armed forces, scientists and shady
government representatives into the story seems more suited to *The X-
Files* than *Buffy the Vampire Slayer*. 'You know, soldiers running
around with big rifles . . .' says Whedon. 'We got to play out all of our
James Bond fantasies, on a slightly smaller budget.'[35] Which may have
been fun to write, but we didn't sign up to see James Bond, which in
terms of genre seems one step too far for a show that gets away with

Professor Maggie Walsh: head of the Initiative

dealing with vampires on a weekly basis. The vampires have always been a part of the Buffyverse and we accept that. James Bond, by contrast, seems like tacked-on science fiction, and the first time in the series that one of its borrowed elements feels out of place.

Maggie Walsh, the psychology professor introduced as the 'Evil Bitch Monster of Death', is a promising addition to the cast of characters. She's prickly, arrogant, clever, ambiguous in her attitude towards Buffy and extremely mean to Giles ('Buffy clearly lacks a strong father figure,' she tells him spitefully), which shows masses of potential for future conflict. Of course, she turns out to be running the Initiative (college teaching jobs, as everyone knows, leaving plenty of leisure time to oversee a complex covert paramilitary operation on the side) and

Adam: half human, half demon, all Big Bad

even attempts to have Buffy killed. *Pace* Faith and Drusilla, up to this point the Big Bads have all been male, and it looks as though there will also be an undercurrent of feminine rivalry in a battle for Riley's affections. But just as Walsh is shaping up to be a worthy opponent, she's bumped off by the season's real Big Bad – a human–demon hybrid called Adam, a Frankenstein's monster with a predilection, like his literary ancestor, for philosophical musing. His encounter with a child in 'Goodbye Iowa' appears to be a direct reference to the monster–child meeting in James Whale's *Frankenstein*. 'What am I?' asks Adam, to which the small boy replies, 'You're a monster,' before being killed off screen. (Even *Buffy the Vampire Slayer* backs away from the explicit deaths of innocent children; the child corpses in Season Three's 'Gingerbread', the discovery of which propels Joyce and other Sunnydale mothers into a vigilante witch-hunt, turn out to be of demonic provenance.) Once one has grasped that Adam is physically and mentally invulnerable, he's not terribly interesting as a character. The potential is there – as we will learn, the Slayer also has a touch of demon in her, and she must draw on this in order to defeat him – but the possibilities of a more personal link between the two are never explored. His motivation seems abstract and impersonal (unlike previous Big Bads, he doesn't seem particularly interested in Buffy) and he ends up as just another demonic ass to be kicked.

Even more damaging to Season Four is the introduction into the Buffy canon of two of its most tiresome figures. Riley Finn, though posing as a student, is actually an Initiative soldier beefed up by steroid-type drugs and artificially created combat skills that enable him to fight alongside the Slayer. (In a plot development that goes nowhere in particular, it's suggested that he, like Adam, is the result of one of Maggie Walsh's experiments, making him Adam's half-brother.) As the season unfolds, Riley becomes Buffy's main romantic interest. Admittedly Angel is a hard act to follow, but Riley isn't sexy, he's not clever and he's certainly not funny; in story terms he's more a pawn than a major player, and finds himself increasingly sidelined in his girlfriend's life before mercifully, halfway through Season Five, a helicopter arrives

The very boring Riley Finn (left)

to whisk him away to battle demons in Belize. All he does is provide the Slayer with someone to date and have sex with. Their relationship doesn't tell us anything we haven't already grasped – that Buffy's looking for someone to depend on, but is going to have trouble finding him because she's a lot stronger, both physically and mentally, than regular human guys. Even with his artificially induced superstrength, Riley can't keep up with her – when they spar, she holds back but still wins easily – and when he's finally deprived of it, he can't cope with his feelings of not measuring up. Perhaps this side of him should have been explored more thoroughly, or even developed into a malign force, but the character is just too vanilla. The most exciting thing he does (and even that didn't exactly keep me glued to my armchair) is in Season Five, when he starts hanging out in the vampire equivalent of crack houses and paying vampire chicks to take nips out of him. Honestly, he's so pathetic that he can't even go all the way and turn into a vampire, which would at least have presented Buffy with the agonising choice of whether to stake or not to stake. Instead, we're not sorry to see the back of this doofus, who's the first but unfortunately not the last character to whinge about not getting enough attention from the Slayer (who by the way has other things on her mind at this point, such as her mother's brain tumour and a rampaging supermalevolent demon-god) in the same way that children and teenagers in Hollywood films invariably whine about not getting enough attention from their parents. Just as you secretly wish these parents would resign from their jobs and give their offspring unlimited quantities of quality time but fewer consumer goods, just to see how the sprogs would like having to construct their own toys out of empty Squeezy bottles and a ball of string (which is how we were forced to amuse ourselves when I was a girl), so it crossed my mind that, yes, Buffy should have given up vampire slaying, let the Big Bad run amok and neglected to visit her mother in hospital in order to spend more quality time with Riley, just to see how he'd like it. Of course he wouldn't; the reason he was drawn to her in the first place was her strength of character, her struggle to do the right thing and commitment to a cause. Without these, she wouldn't be Buffy.

Meanwhile, Willow and Oz, after the better part of two seasons in each other's company, have split up. There is low-key foreshadowing of the rupture in the second episode of the season when Oz shares an unspoken 'moment' with a passing chick who later turns out to be a werewolf; nothing is made of this at the time, but it so reminded me of the brief scene in Jacques Tourneur's *Cat People* (1943) in which the anti-heroine encounters another 'cat person' that I instantly guessed what was coming. Sure enough, Oz later has uninhibited weresex with the weregirl, and although later, still in wolfish guise, he kills her when she threatens Willow, the awareness that he cannot control his wilder urges drives him away from Sunnydale in search of ways to harness his inner beastliness.

Willow and her werewolf boyfriend, Oz

Willow is so heartbroken it takes her all of three episodes to find a replacement – not to mention change her sexual orientation – when she takes up with Tara, a timid fellow wiccan. The novelty of a lesbian couple in a mainstream American TV series aimed at teenagers initially blinds us to the fact that Tara, like Riley, is dead weight. The problem here is perhaps the writers' reluctance to paint a lesbian relationship in anything other than a positive light, or to insinuate in any way that lesbianism might be a deep dark secret on a par with, say, Giles's delinquent past. Willow swaps teams with a remarkable lack of soul-searching, her early doubts about presenting her new girlfriend to the other Scoobies are easily quashed and her friends accept this new development with an insouciance bordering on indifference. (I'm not

saying they should have been antagonistic, just a little more surprised.)
After a hint that there may be more to Tara than meets the eye (unseen
by Willow, she deliberately sabotages a demon-locating spell, suggesting
there might be something demonic about her), we give her the benefit of
the doubt until the hint is exposed as a dishonest tease in a touchy-feely
episode called 'Family' in Season Five, a rare Whedon-penned misfire in
which it's revealed that she's not a demon after all – just, yeuch, a young
woman with an overbearing father.

The relationship between Willow and Tara is all sweetness and
light, peace and love, hand-holding and wicca spells and, like Tara
herself, off-puttingly New Agey. Their conversations don't seem to be
about anything, though since they had a tendency to send me to sleep,

Willow and Tara: the Diane and Diane problem

I'm prepared to admit I might have missed something. Typical of their banter is a scene in which the two of them sit on a roof and have a conversation about the stars; Willow points out Cassopeia and Tara responds with her own pet names for the constellations, starting with the Big Pineapple . . . Oh no, it's too ghastly. Willow and Tara talk because they're together, not because they have anything of interest to say; no writer worth his or her salt would dream of making a heterosexual relationship this inconsequential. In a theoretically admirable attempt to be politically correct, Team Whedon has broken its own rule: Willow and Tara are the new Sam and Diane, or rather Diane and Diane. Things look up for a while at the end of Season Five when the Big Bad drains Tara's brain, but I'm afraid one's natural response is to quote Dorothy Parker on the death of President Coolidge – 'How can they tell?' – since the character's slack-jawed gaze and droopy dress sense have already made her seem semi-retarded. Alas, she recovers and continues to blight the series with her tie-dyed boho chic and melting spaniel eyes and soft-spoken feminine wisdom until she's dispatched by a stray bullet at the end of Season Six, thus putting us out of our misery. Had it been Giles or Xander or even Willow shot dead, I might have been upset, but I was only too thankful to see the back of Tara. She's little more than a cypher, a poster-girl for positive lesbianism. Unlike the core characters, she has no hidden depths and never develops beyond our first glimpse of her. In the Buffyverse, she's nothing but filler.

91

Fortunately, the deadening effect of Riley and Tara is partially offset by the reintroduction of two old favourites, who are all set to develop in new and interesting ways. The behaviour-altering chip in Spike's brain turns him into the vampire equivalent of a eunuch, unable to achieve dental penetration. Thus neutered, he starts hanging out with the Scoobies and skewering moments of potential mushiness with cynical quips, replacing Cordelia as the disruptive element in the gang. Best of all, he's mercenary and still not to be trusted, which makes his presence an enjoyable wild card. Spike is like Loki of the Norse legends or Q of *Star Trek: The Next Generation* – someone who likes to stir things up, just for the hell of it. Best of all, there are further, major changes ahead for him. Of all the characters in the Buffyverse, he's the one who undergoes the most radical transformation, and it's his emotional journey that provides the final three seasons with much of their forward thrust.

The other new kid on the block is Anya, the 1,000-year-old ex-vengeance demon who is still coming to terms with being trapped in a mortal body. Her skewed attempts at normal conversation and behaviour, Martian-like observation of her own unfamiliar emotions provide a running note of comedy, while her monumental lack of tact is also reminiscent of Cordelia. (When Giles announces he has a friend coming to town, Anya says, 'You mean an orgasm friend?' to which

Anya Emerson, ex-vengeance demon

Giles replies, 'Yes, that's exactly the most appalling thing you could have said.') But the ever-present possibility that she might revert to her old vengeance demon ways (as indeed she eventually does) gives her a dangerous and unpredictable edge that prevents her from ever becoming too kooky and irritating.

Faith too makes an all-too-brief comeback before exiting stage-left for further guest appearances on *Angel*, jail-time, redemption and an eventual guest slot in *Buffy the Vampire Slayer*'s final showdown. Amid all this coming and going, Season Four flails around, trying to find its footing but mostly falling back on retreads of old ideas. There are demons-of-the-week (Buffy's room-mate, the vengeful spirits of massacred Native Americans, the evil director of a children's home)

The Gentlemen: 'Nosferatu meets *Hellraiser* by way of The Joker'

and a recycling of tried-and-tested formulae (haunted frat houses, Halloween, worst fears made manifest, spells-gone-wrong), but what's lacking is a compelling narrative arc to link them all together. Instead, the highlights of Season Four are gimmicky one-off episodes written and directed by Joss Whedon (though he's too smart not to weave in threads of character development). Having been told that his forte was dialogue, Whedon perversely decided to dispense with it altogether for the genuinely eerie 'Hush', in which Sunnydale is invaded by the Gentlemen – one of whom is described in the original teleplay as, 'Nosferatu meets *Hellraiser* by way of the Joker. Actually he looks kind of like Mr Burns, except that he can't stop his rictus grin, and his teeth are gleaming metal.'[36] The Gentlemen are nattily dressed fairy-tale bogeymen – reminiscent of the aliens in *Dark City* – who steal the voices of the townsfolk. At least half of this episode passes in silent-movie mode, with the Scoobies forced to converse through mime and scribbled messages, with hilarious results. 'When you stop talking, you start communicating,'[37] says Whedon, who built the whole episode into a *tour de force* on the subject of communication, or lack of it.

94

Whedon's second *tour de force* rounds off the weakest season in the series with an unusual and encouraging flourish to replace the now traditional saving the world (in this case the final showdown with Adam, which was brought forward into the penultimate episode). 'I thought it would be nice to do something very different,'[38] says Whedon, who conceived the idea of an episode constructed almost entirely out of the dreams of the Core Four. Exhausted after the battle against Adam and his army, Buffy, Giles, Willow and Xander retire to Buffy's house to chill out. But no sooner have they settled down to watch a batch of videos (including the aptly titled *Apocalypse Now*) than they fall asleep.

Dream sequences are a favourite narrative device of *Buffy the Vampire Slayer*. From a writer's point of view, they provide a convenient way of injecting a shock-horror moment into a slow build-up (a preview of coming attractions, as it were, as when Buffy dreams about the Gentlemen in the pre-credits teaser to 'Hush') or of providing

visual clues about a character's fears, as when Angel's dream of Buffy
bursting into flames on the steps of a church indicates he knows their
relationship is doomed. Buffy's dreams are often prophetic; in Season
One she dreams about being defeated by the Master; in Season Two, her
troubled dreams provide an ominous foreshadowing of Angel's
transformation into Angelus, while at the end of Season Three, it's
thanks to a dream about Faith that she is finally able to defeat the
Mayor.

'Restless' is unusual, however, in that the dreams form the
backbone of the narrative. (Coincidentally, an episode of *The Sopranos*
aired a few weeks earlier had used dream sequences to resolve an
important plot point in the season finale.) 'I was basically sitting down
to write a forty-minute tone poem,' says Whedon. He thought, 'a nice
coda to the season' would be

> to just do a piece that commented on all of the four main characters
> that we'd grown to know and love, and where they were in their lives
> and what they felt about things and each other. So we built the
> structure based on the idea of dreams – one dream per act . . . the
> running thread in all of them being that they would be attacked by the
> spirit of the First Slayer, the Primitive.[39]

95

'I literally just had to make it flow and make sure the images were true to
the characters. Anything goes so long as it doesn't look like a trick.'[40]
The results are authentically dreamlike in the way they shuffle familiar
characters and locations, pop culture references (a production of *Death
of a Salesman* that bears no relation to the actual play; Principal Snyder
popping up in the Captain Kurtz role from *Apocalypse Now*), sexual
fantasies (mostly Xander's) and a scattering of visual and verbal non-
sequiturs. Whedon uses non-naturalistic techniques such as obvious
back-projection, over-exposed footage and unnatural colour, but there's
a marked lack of the clichés traditionally used in dream sequences, such

as dry ice, floaty slow motion or (qv *Twin Peaks*) dwarves. Everything is presented in a matter-of-fact way that accurately reflects dream logic.

Each dream provides fascinating insights into the dreamer's (and Whedon's) psyche, with tension added by the sinister presence of the First Slayer, who attacks and appears to kill Willow, Xander and Giles in their sleep, but it's Buffy's dream that virtually lays the foundation for everything that will happen in Season Five. Joyce is living behind a wall in the school corridor (the image of her face peering out from the broken plaster echoes a similar shot in Season Two's 'School Hard'), suggesting there will shortly be a large obstacle (and you can't get much larger than death) between her and her daughter. Tara tells Buffy, 'Be back before Dawn', and in Season Five we'll be meeting a

The First Slayer: 'Just the kill. We are alone'

character with that very name. Riley is wearing a suit and talking about world domination, suggesting Buffy's increasing emotional distance from him.

Eventually, she emerges into a brightly lit desert landscape where Tara acts as translator in a showdown with the First Slayer, a dark-skinned warrior woman with snaky dreadlocks, mud-smeared face and limbs wrapped in unravelling Mummylike strips of fabric. The First Slayer takes her calling very seriously. 'I have no speech, no name, other than the action of death, the blood cry, the penetrating wound. I am destruction absolute, alone.'

'The Slayer does not walk in the world,' says Tara/First Slayer, but we know from experience that Buffy doesn't respond well to pompous pronouncements, and she responds with a surreal version of her manifesto: 'I walk, I talk, I shop, I sneeze . . . There's trees in the desert since you moved out, and I don't sleep on a bed of bones. Now give me back my friends.'

'No friends,' says the First Slayer. 'Just the kill. We are alone.' The moment is intense and a little scary. But just then the Cheese Man pops up to remind Buffy that she's dreaming, and she declares, 'That's it. I'm waking up.' Unlike previous Slayers, she is *not* alone, and that is her strength.

Apart from the First Slayer, the element common to all four dreams is the Cheese Man, an odd little bald guy who makes peculiar remarks about the cheese slices he's displaying. 'He's the only thing that has no meaning,' says Whedon.[41] The word 'cheese' has a host of slang definitions (many of them connected to smegma and masturbation, which we'll pass over here) but perhaps it's a manifestation of Whedon's subconscious idea that, although he is obviously proud of *Buffy the Vampire Slayer*, he is nevertheless working in a mix of genres (teen and horror stories) that are despised by high-minded critics who might have difficulty accepting the show as anything other than 'cheesy'.

7 Death and the Maiden

What Happens in Season Five

Giles rediscovers purpose in his life by buying the magic shop, which
will henceforth serve as HQ for the Scoobies. Joyce has a fainting fit and
goes into hospital for tests. Buffy is shocked to find out that her
annoying little sister Dawn is, in fact, a mystical and non-corporeal Key

Glory aka Glorificus

Glory's alter ego: Ben, the friendly intern

sent to her in human form by an order of monks as a desperate ploy to
stop it falling into the hands of the season's Big Bad. This turns out to be
an incredibly ancient god called Glorificus whose human form switches
between Glory, a spoilt Californian Valley Girl-type, and Ben, a
sympathetic intern at the hospital where Joyce is being treated. Buffy
finds she's no match for Glory, who bests her in combat without raising
a sweat, but (after Riley's departure) feels attracted to Ben, whose
connection to the Big Bad is revealed to the Scoobies only at the end of
the season.

      Riley, feeling increasingly marginalised in Buffy's life, starts
hanging around in vampire bars and finally (hurrah!) leaves town.
Dawn, who has been programmed with a full complement of memories
about life with Buffy and Joyce, is as shocked as everyone else to
discover she is not human. Joyce's operation to remove a brain tumour
appears to be a success, but she later dies. Spike has a vivid erotic dream
about Buffy and realises to his horror that he has fallen in love with her,
though she and the other Scoobies continue to despise him. When

99

Drusilla and Harmony return to Sunnydale, he rejects them both, and forces Warren, a geek with advanced technological capabilities, to build him a robot Buffy lookalike, henceforth known as the 'Buffybot'.

Buffy learns more about her Slayer heritage; every Slayer has a death wish, and her gift is Death. In her search for the Key, Glory drains Tara's brain and leaves her a drooling idiot; a vengeful Willow goes all black-eyed and witchy and counter-attacks with telekinetically launched knives, but her magic is not strong enough to defeat Glorificus. The Scoobies, realising they're helpless against such a powerful entity, flee into the desert where they're attacked by Knights of the Byzantium, who want to destroy Dawn before Glory can use her blood to open a portal between dimensions, thus bringing about the End of the World. Giles is seriously injured, so Buffy calls on Ben for help, but as soon as the intern arrives he morphs into Glory, slaughters the besieging knights and kidnaps Dawn. Buffy retreats into a guilt-induced catatonic state of shock but, with some mind-melding help from Willow, snaps out of it just in time for the Big Showdown. Willow restores Tara's brain, Giles quietly kills Ben (thus destroying Glory as well) and Buffy sacrifices herself (by jumping off a tower of scaffolding) to seal the portal and save her sister. The inscription on her gravestone reads:

Buffy Anne Summers
1981–2001
Beloved Sister
Devoted Friend
She Saved the World
A Lot.

The introduction of Buffy's sister Dawn is an outrageous *coup de télévision*, so cleverly conceived and executed that it never feels like a cheat, unlike the end of the 1985–6 season of *Dallas* when Bobby (whom we had all thought dead) steps out of the shower – and the entire season is dismissed as a dream. *Buffy the Vampire Slayer* has an advantage over such series, of course, in that the Buffyverse has from the

'Death is your gift'

outset relinquished all claims to any realism other than psychological and emotional. In the first episode of Season Five, Dawn is not introduced as a new character (Buffy's long-lost stepsister, say, who'd been living with relatives on the other side of the country) but as someone who has always been there, living alongside Buffy and Joyce. She's in all the family photos. She has a bedroom of her own, filled with her belongings. Only brain-damaged hospital patients (and Joyce, when her tumour kicks in) suspect there's anything unusual about her, until Buffy – and the viewers – learn the truth in the season's fifth episode. After her early suspicions are dispelled, Buffy realises that Dawn is an innocent pawn who must henceforth be accepted as her flesh-and-blood sister, as does everyone else when they also find out the truth. Dawn is here to stay, alas, and she continues to whinge and whine all the way through Seasons Six and Seven when all this business about her being the Key is long forgotten.

But Dawn performs a key function (pun intended) in the story arc of Season Five. After Joyce's death, she also provides Buffy

with a family tie (Mr Summers, in Spain with his secretary, maintains
radio silence even during his ex-wife's illness), forcing the Slayer to
grow up and act as a responsible guardian, though whether or not she
needs family (Giles has always been her surrogate father, while Xander
and Willow have been as good as siblings) is a moot point. Dawn also
takes over from the increasingly self-sufficient Scoobies as a vulnerable
character who needs to be rescued at regular intervals. Perhaps the
writers were also aware that the Core Four were ageing (Giles has
always been over the hill, but Buffy celebrates her twentieth birthday
in Season Five) and that a younger character was required to retain the
interest of the show's target audience. All this is well and good, but it
doesn't stop Dawn from being a gigantic pain in the ass. Even by little
sister standards, she's whiny, squealy, clingy, forever complaining
about not getting enough attention and repeatedly puts not just herself
but everyone else in jeopardy by her stupidity – for example, by
inviting vampires into the house, or by throwing a hissy fit and running
away whenever there are dangerous demons on the loose, making her
even more of a liability than Riley or Tara. Unlike Buffy, who was

102

Buffy's annoying little sister, Dawn

little more than Dawn's age when first forced to confront her vampire-slaying legacy, Dawn never seems to learn from her mistakes and by the time her character finally starts to grow up, towards the end of Season Seven, it's too late. We hate her. She's the Violet Elizabeth *de nos jours*.

Death is a moveable feast in the Buffyverse. One of the advantages of a show with a supernatural theme, and one of the recurring tropes of the series, is, 'Just because you die doesn't mean you're dead.'[42] Buffy dies (and is brought back to life) at the end of Season One. Angel (who was dead long before the series began) is comprehensively dispatched (or so it appeared) at the end of Season Two, only to bounce back hunkier than ever in Season Three. Week after week, characters die and return as vampires, often to die yet again when Buffy stakes them. Others return as zombies or ghosts. But Season Five tackles the subject of death head-on by addressing the natural demise of a recurring supporting character – Buffy's mother, Joyce. The theme of mortality has already been introduced in 'Fool for Love', when Buffy takes her eye off the ball while patrolling and a vampire turns her own stake against her. Shaken by the

103

Spike in his pre-vampire incarnation as William the poet

near-miss, she tries to dig up information on the deaths of previous Slayers and ends up having to approach the only person she knows with first-hand experience of the subject – Spike, who has killed two Slayers in his long career and who, in Season Two at least, had been hoping to add Buffy to the score.

'Fool for Love' is a flashback episode (filmed in tandem with 'Darla', an episode in Season Two of *Angel* which presents many of the same events from Angel's point of view). In London, 1880, we meet Spike in his pre-vampire incarnation as William, a wilting Victorian who writes terrible poetry and is humiliated by Cecily, the woman he loves. We see the disconsolate William being sired by the vampire Drusilla, who's in town with fellow vampires Angel and Darla. We see Spike squabbling with Angel, killing one Slayer during the Boxer Rebellion in 1900 and another on the New York City subway in 1977. During the latter flashback, Spike turns to the camera to address us, and Buffy, directly. 'Every Slayer has a death wish,' he says. 'Part of you wants it.' And we see Spike in 1998 in South America, splitting up with Drusilla, who with her precognitive powers is already aware of something he's not – that his obsession with Buffy is more than about just killing her. The episode comes full circle with Spike making a pass at Buffy, who rejects him with an echo of Cecily's scornful words, 'You're beneath me'. The lessons Buffy learns in this episode are put into practice at the end of the season, and the words of the First Slayer – 'Death is your gift' – are interpreted literally when she sacrifices herself to save the world and (my impassioned yell of 'For God's sake, let them take Dawn instead!' going unheeded) her annoying little sister in particular.

Despite constant rejection, Spike continues to moon over Buffy and even proves himself a useful member of the Scoobies, babysitting Dawn when occasion demands it and refusing, under torture, to betray her to the Big Bad. He still provides the show with a running patter of acerbic comments, but now we are able to glimpse a tragic side to him as well – he's the embodiment of the idea that inside every cynical tough guy lurks a squishy romantic. In undead terms, and despite his bad boy attitude and all the atrocities he has committed throughout his bloodsucking career, Spike has never been a terribly successful vampire; he has always let sentiment get the better of him, and his actions are often personally motivated, rather than pure evil just for the hell of it. (The Judge spots this in Season Two when he says to Spike and Dru, 'You two stink of humanity. You share affection and jealousy.') With Spike's bloodlust neutralised by the chip in his brain, it's only logical that his obsession with the Slayer should veer from passionate hatred to passionate love, and that he should strive to be worthy of the object of his desire so that, ultimately, he *chooses* to be a good guy, even after the chip is finally removed in Season Seven.

Joss Whedon dropped in to write and direct 'The Body', an episode that stands out as atypical in tone and content in a series that normally deals with death in what Whedon describes as 'a fantastic and often jokey way'.[43] This is very different from all the stakings and explosions and gloopy demon deaths to which we've grown accustomed. Joyce dies from natural causes (an aneurism – 'a sudden haemorrhage from a ruptured arterial vessel near where the tumour was removed') and Buffy can't do a thing about it. Seriousness of purpose is signalled by absence of the 'Previously on *Buffy the Vampire Slayer*' montage at the

105

The death of Joyce Summers

beginning, absence of background music and long faces all round, and though Buffy stakes a vampire at the end of the episode, just to remind us that we're not watching *ER*, the overall tone is very po-faced, as though everyone concerned is convinced they're making Very Important Television.

Coincidentally, the same year as Joyce's death in 2001, the hospital soap opera *ER* also had a brain tumour thread affecting a central character, Dr Mark Greene. Even more coincidentally, this was the year in which my own mother was diagnosed with, and eventually died from, an inoperable brain tumour. Oddly, although during her illness I watched episodes from both TV shows, it never struck me that these fictional characters were suffering from a condition bearing any resemblance to hers. Perhaps my subconscious was diligently separating fact from fiction, and stubbornly refused to view TV shows, however unflinching their approach, as anything other than escapist entertainment. Or perhaps I was in shock, or denial. At any rate, the first time I watched 'The Body', it left me cold – I couldn't wait for Buffy to get back to her regular vampire-staking routine. It was only when reviewing it several years later that I realised how accurately it captured the downright strangeness of bereavement: the dislocation, lack of melodrama, the routines and rituals that are unfamiliar yet mundane, the not knowing the correct way to talk or behave, the tendency of grief to manifest itself through overreaction to trivial and apparently unconnected events, the nagging awareness that although everything seems to be going on as normal, life will never be the same again. 'The Body' is painful to watch, but only because the subject matter is so grim, and the various reactions of the Scoobies – Willow obsessing over what to wear, Xander's search for someone to blame and Anya's bewilderment – all ring emotionally true. The ex-vengeance demon makes her usual tactless comments before breaking down and crying,

> But I don't understand. I don't understand how all this happens, how we
> go through this. I mean, I knew her and then she's, there's just a body,
> and I don't understand why she can't just get back in it and not be dead.

Despite moments such as this, 'The Body' is scrupulous in its avoidance of the sort of lachrymose wallowing to be found in, say, an episode of *Joan of Arcadia*, in which a mortally wounded recurring character fades away in her hospital bed amid an orgy of snivelling and maudlin violins. It's painful to watch all right, but only because the process seems interminable, and you can't wait for her to die.

Buffy's death in the last episode of the season is of a different order to that of her mother. By the time British viewers got to see 'The Gift', there can have been few who were not privy (thanks to trailers, magazines, websites and, in my case, a loose-lipped chum) to the information that Buffy was going to die, with the result that the Slayer's ultimate sacrifice isn't nearly as shocking as it might have been prior to the 'Who Shot JR?' media frenzy in the early 1980s, after which future developments in TV series began to leak into newspapers and magazines on a regular basis. But then, since the whole of Season Five has been building inexorably to Buffy's realisation that the line, 'Death is your gift', has more than one meaning, what happens is almost an anti-climax.

107

Buffy is dead. She had a good innings: five seasons, with over a hundred vampires staked on screen, and (one suspects) many more between episodes. The show could have ended there – but magazines and websites had already indicated that it was due to return, albeit on another American TV network. Joss Whedon had fallen out with WB executive Jamie Kellner, who had publicly dissed *Buffy the Vampire Slayer* by calling it a teen show (which it was, of course, though his comments were evidently not intended as a compliment) and telling *Entertainment Weekly*, 'It's not our number one show. It's not a show like *ER* that stands above the pack.'[44]

He was wrong of course. One suspects that Buffy will be remembered long after Doctors Greene, Carter and Ross have been consigned to the mists of TV history.

8 Revenge of the Nerds

What Happens in Season Six

After Buffy's death, Giles goes back to England. With the help of the
Buffybot, the remaining Scoobies continue to fight vampires in
Sunnydale. Willow enlists Xander, Tara and Anya to help her cast a
resurrection spell to bring Buffy back from what they assume is a hell
dimension similar to the one where Angel was trapped between Seasons
Two and Three. The spell succeeds, but Buffy, after clawing her way out
of her coffin, seems subdued; only later do her friends learn they didn't
save her from hell, but snatched her out of heaven. Giles returns to see
her, but soon goes back to England. Buffy finds it hard adjusting to daily
life and is forced to take on a series of badly paid jobs in a bid to ease her
financial problems. Unknown to the others, she also embarks on an
intense physical relationship with Spike, who alone is able to relate to
her life-after-death experiences.

Everyone else has problems of their own. Willow becomes
dangerously addicted to magic, and Tara leaves her. Dawn becomes a
kleptomaniac. Xander and Anya get engaged, but on the day of their
wedding Xander jilts her at the altar, propelling her back into her old
vengeance demon ways. Buffy is disgusted by her sexual dependence on
Spike and breaks up with him. After attempting to rape her, he travels
to Africa in what appears to be yet another attempt to get his chip
removed; after many trials, the chip remains but his soul is restored.

The season's Big Bad is a trio of nerds called Warren, Jonathan and Andrew. To begin with, they're little more than a thorn in the Slayer's side, but Warren, after accidentally killing his ex-girlfriend, becomes unstable and more dangerous. After Buffy humiliates him in a fight, he gets his revenge by shooting her. Tara and Willow get back together, only for Tara to be killed by a stray bullet from Warren's gun. Willow's bid to resurrect her dead girlfriend fails and she turns all black-eyed and witchy; after healing Buffy's wound, she tracks down Warren, whom she tortures and flays. She is only stopped from doing the same to Andrew and Jonathan by the intervention of the other Scoobies. The two surviving nerds flee to Mexico. Buffy and Willow fight; just as it looks as though Willow is going to kick Buffy's ass, Giles turns up, armed with magic borrowed from a coven in Devon. He holds Willow at bay, but she breaks free, drains him of his power, traps Buffy and Dawn in a big hole in the cemetery and prepares to bring about the End of the World. At the last minute, Xander talks her out of it by reminding her she's still his best friend and that he will always love her, come what may.

A hero's career invariably ends in glorious death, which also solves the little problem of what to do with him afterwards. Can you imagine Achilles, the golden warrior, settling down with a nice young man to lead a life of domestic bliss? Or a repentant Guinevere nursing a wounded Arthur back to life and the two of them growing old together? Or Odin and Thor consulting with architects on how best to rebuild Valhalla? The life of heroes who survive the big showdown with death is inevitably filled with anti-climax, pain and bitterness; Hercules' attempt to live happily ever after ends in ignominious death by poisoned tunic. Agamemnon survives the Trojan war only to be hacked to pieces by his wife (or, according to the makers of the film *Troy* [2004], stabbed to death by a slavegirl). In *Robin and Marian* (1976), the only solution Marian can offer the ageing hero is low-key murder–suicide. It's nobler and more dignified, from the hero's point of view, to go out with a big bang, or at the very least, ride off into the sunset like Shane or Mad

Max, never to be seen again, but immortalised in the songs and stories of the ordinary folk they've left behind.

It was always conceivable, of course, that *Buffy the Vampire Slayer* could have continued without Buffy, the absence of the title character being no impediment to the continuation of TV series such as the Glasgow-set crime series *Taggart* (1985–), which continued long after the death of its lead actor, Mark McManus, while the character of Roj Blake went MIA for the last two seasons of *Blake's 7*, only reappearing in time to be killed off along with everyone else in the final episode. But there was no hint on the media grapevine that Sarah Michelle Gellar had thrown in the towel, and since Buffy's death, unlike that of Joyce, had been mystical (normally, leaping off the top of that scaffolding would have merely stunned her – she's survived worse – and her corpse was markedly unbroken and unbloodied), it leaves the way open for Willow's resurrection spell, which also, incidentally, shows just how radically Willow has changed from the sweet-natured nerd of Season One. The Willow of Season Six slits the throat of a Bambi-like fawn without a qualm, and seems only mildly disconcerted when, during the resurrection ceremony, a large snake emerges from her mouth.

By now, Joss Whedon was not only juggling *Buffy* and *Angel* duties, but also developing a new TV series called *Firefly*. But he dropped in long enough to provide Season Six – and the entire series – with one of its most memorable episodes. In 'Once More, with Feeling', the demon-of-the-week (inadvertently conjured by Xander) afflicts citizens of Sunnydale with a compulsion to sing and, like the heroine of Hans Christian Andersen's *The Red Shoes*, dance – until they literally go up in smoke. This episode was shot in MGM-style widescreen, with the usual credit sequence replaced by an orchestral overture, and the regular characters compelled to blurt out their innermost secrets in song. Meanwhile, Sunnydale's townsfolk are hoofing their hearts out in the background, trilling about the joys of dry cleaning, pleading tunefully with traffic wardens or, after the discovery of the first charred corpse, giving witness arias to the police.

It's an outrageous gimmick, if not quite as original as its fans might have us believe. As far back as 1966, an episode of *Gilligan's Island* featured the characters putting on a musical version of *Hamlet*, while the 'Atomic Shakespeare' episode of *Moonlighting* was a black-and-white musical daydream version of the show that recast its two main characters as Petruchio and Kate from *The Taming of the Shrew*. Characters in *The Simpsons* regularly burst into song, a habit commemorated in the clip show, 'All Singing, All Dancing'.

In 'Once More, with Feeling', the musical numbers (written and composed, of course, by Whedon, with a little help from Christophe Beck) are parodies of different musical styles – romantic ballads, rock anthems and so on – like the songs in *Phantom of the Paradise* (1974), *The Rocky Horror Picture Show* (1975), even Disney movies. But what makes the episode work so beautifully is the way the songs comment on and develop the season's story arcs. It's here that Buffy reveals to the other Scoobies that when they resurrected her, they dragged her out of heaven, not hell. Xander and Anya give musical voice to their doubts about the forthcoming nuptials; Giles realises in song that he's going to have to leave the country again if Buffy is to learn to stand on her own two feet; Tara sings that Willow has cast a spell on her, unaware it's not just metaphorical; and right at the end, in true musical comedy style, Buffy and Spike lock lips in their very first kiss.

The all-singing, all-dancing 'Once More, with Feeling'

With Season Six, the writers of *Buffy the Vampire Slayer* were faced with a choice. Either they could go on repeating the tried and tested formula – demon-of-the-week episodes interwoven with the build-up to the showdown with a powerful Big Bad – or they could risk upsetting fans by breaking the mould and trying something new. Buffy had already survived death; now, Season Six featured life itself as the Big Bad. The recurring villains are more catalysts than a viable menace; the real threats come from within the characters themselves, left to their own devices without an adult chaperone now that their real or surrogate parents have either died or flown back to England. In Season Six, bad things happen to good people.

It didn't always come off. The delicate balance between sitcom, teen drama, action adventure and horror was disrupted, and some of the season's longueurs can be traced to demon-of-the-week storylines being shunted aside by soap opera. Some fans were alienated by changes that made their beloved characters less than loveable ('Series Six is an abomination'[45]), but there were also those of us who appreciated the show's determination not to remain stuck in a rut, like *The X-Files*, from which I bailed long before its ninth and final season, fed up with the way, week after week, Mulder would continue to believe in the paranormal while Scully, repeatedly denying the evidence in front of her own eyes, would remain sceptical.

Despite the obligatory witty dialogue, Season Six is even darker in tone than the death-themed Season Five. Buffy is trapped in a state of post-resurrection depression, unable to connect on an emotional level with her old friends. How can she, when she's lost her mother, died and been snatched out of heaven – experiences the other Scoobies cannot begin to comprehend? Little wonder she turns to Spike for comfort, leading to a relationship, dubbed 'Spuffy', that became another point of contention for certain fans, who complained about its physicality (the first time Buffy and Spike have sex, their foreplay literally brings the house down) and declared it a pale parody of the Buffy–Angel romance, as though all slayer–vampire couplings should be carbon-copies of each other. Whereas with Angel, and to a lesser degree Riley, Buffy had idealised romantic relationships, with Spike it's pure

The birth of 'Spuffy': Buffy and Spike's first kiss

lust – at least from her point of view. Ironically, it's Spike who seeks more intimacy and, when Buffy finally rejects him in an access of self-loathing, he tries to force himself on her. Once again, some fans were upset by the attempted rape; they'd forgotten that, though Spike had a behaviour-modifying chip and funny dialogue and was generally cool, he was still a soulless vampire, and therefore evil by definition. Me, I was more upset by Buffy's cold-hearted treatment of him prior to the assault; it's not until Season Seven that she admits to having been 'a monster'. This Buffy is no longer the bright-eyed cheerleader type who arrived at Sunnydale High and had a cute one-liner for every occasion. She's still a long way from the cynical, battle-scarred Buffy depicted in 'The Wish', but in Season Six she treats Spike with a coldness and condescension worthy of Cordelia at her queen-bitchiest. As Whedon remarked à propos of Season Two, 'the scariest thing on the show was people behaving badly, or in peril, morally speaking . . .'[46] At this stage in the series, when we're aware that Buffy is capable of bouncing back from just about any physical threat that fate can throw at her – including the big one, death – it's her less than adorable behaviour rather than any extraneous menace that makes us fearful on her behalf. It's her humanity, her very *soul*, in peril now.

113

But then dying is easy and living is hard, as Buffy finds out to her cost. It's not unheard of for dead heroes to be resurrected, but they rarely linger long on this earthly plane, and certainly not to engage in real life on a daily basis: Jesus ascends into heaven, Hercules ascends to Olympus and, according to some legends, Arthur and his knights are not dead but sleeping, awaiting the call to arms. No such cop-out for Buffy – not only does she have to contend with the trauma of having been ripped out of heaven (her memory of it is hazy, an abstract impression of peace, with no mention of God or angels) but Joyce's medical expenses have left her daughters in a precarious financial situation. The bank manager remarks that, 'For some reason, property values in Sunnydale have never been competitive', which rules out the option of selling the house. But burst pipes, plumber's bills and repeatedly having to repair or replace fixtures and fittings after demon-of-the-week brawling all take their toll on the Summers' purse. 'I've trashed this house so many times,' Buffy reflects. 'How did Mom pay for this?'

And so she has to go where few heroes have ventured before her – into the job market. Earning a living is a subject broached in few heroic fantasies other than, perhaps, superhero comics. Despite working as a photographer, Spider-Man is so broke he can't stump up for an air ticket to Florida; even Superman has to work for a living at the *Daily Planet*, though admittedly that's as much to provide him with an alias as an income. The hero's 'job' is fighting, not foraging for food. It's his job to clear the way so that *the others* – the ordinary folk – can forage without being robbed or killed. The samurai's 'job' is to rid the village of marauding bandits so the villagers can carrying on planting and harvesting rice; the surviving samurai don't stick around to plant and harvest alongside them. Mad Max's 'job' is to protect the settlers as they set off down the road to a new civilisation; you don't see him tagging along as a motor mechanic.

Due to supernatural interference, Buffy's first forays into the world of work – at Xander's construction site and in the magic shop – end in disaster. She ends up with the classic McJob – slinging burgers at a fast-food joint called Doublemeat Palace. 'She's going to have crap jobs all her life,' says Dawn, 'minimum wage stuff.' And until Season Seven, it looks as though little sister is right.

Throughout the series, the Big Bads have been getting stronger – vampires, demons, gods, defeated only at huge emotional cost and self-sacrifice. Where do we go from here? In Season Six, instead of conjuring an even more powerful adversary – and what could be more powerful than Glorificus? – the series does a cunning little backflip and comes up with the Trio. Warren, Jonathan and Andrew are not so much Big Bads as three Big Bad wannabes who provide much-needed light relief in a season when the darkness is provided by the Scoobies themselves. The Trio's obsession with the minutiae of *Star Wars* and other cult TV and films effectively makes them surrogate *Buffy* fans (in an alternative alternative universe, as it were, *Buffy the Vampire Slayer* would be one of their favourite TV shows) and might well be one of the reasons for the hostility felt by many actual fans towards Season Six. Warren, Jonathan and Andrew are too close to home for comfort. They're the Revenge of the Nerds.

The word 'nerd' originated in the US in the 1950s to denote, 'An unpleasant, insignificant or dull person,' but was marginally redefined in the 1970s to mean, 'Anyone outside a peer group and who thus fails to fit in with "the gang", esp a studious individual who eschews

The Trio: the revenge of the nerds

drink, drugs and similar teen pleasures.'[47] *Revenge of the Nerds* is the title of a mildly subversive 1984 teen movie in which the unlovely losers strike back at the good-looking but heartless jocks and cheerleaders who've been victimising them. Unlike Xander and Willow, the nerds in that film (like the main characters in the short-lived post-*Buffy* TV series *Freaks and Geeks* [1999–]) really do look nerdy – not just bespectacled and swotty and goofy but also spotty and socially maladroit and given to cringe-making laughter. (Their outsider status, however, doesn't stop them spying on naked co-eds or treating women as sex objects.)

Until recently, nerds were a relatively invisible phenomenon. But then came the Internet. Developed by nerds for nerds (and it can be argued that it's really only nerds who fully grasp its technical complexities), the Internet provided them with a hitherto unimaginable platform, tool and mode of expression. In the land of the Internet, the nerd is king. When Peter Jackson declared after his *Lord of the Rings* Oscar triumph, 'The geeks shall inherit the earth', he might as well have been referring to Bill Gates or Steve Jobs, billion-dollar proof that obsessive tinkering with computers can pay off.

Buffy the Vampire Slayer was one of the first TV series to consolidate its popularity through the Internet. Type 'Buffy the Vampire Slayer' into Google and, at the time of writing, you will be rewarded with 1,940,000 results. Type just 'Buffy' and the number leaps to 8,930,000 (some of which, though one suspects not many, will refer to Buffy Saint-Marie, Buffy's Brewery or the Buffy-Headed Marmoset, an endangered species of arboreal monkey found in the Atlantic coastal forests of Brazil). 'Sarah Michelle Gellar' will get you 750,000 hits, 'Joss Whedon' will get you 25,400, and even a supporting demon called d'Hoffryn, who features in no more than a couple of episodes, gets a healthy 8,190.

To browse these websites can be a sobering experience. While many Buffy fans have contributed witty, perceptive analyses of the show and its subtexts, you can also find plenty of 'fan fiction' sites, where aficionados have posted stories they themselves have written about their favourite characters, often with copious amounts of sex, violence or romantic yearning, but seldom showing much understanding of what made these characters tick in the first place; explicit sexual fantasies involving Spike and Buffy are a favourite subject, but there's more than one site dedicated to dodgy encounters between Buffy and Giles ('Surely she couldn't be getting turned on by Giles, of all people . . . Whoa, look at that bulge in his trousers'[48]). Elsewhere, entire forums are dedicated to bitching about the behaviour of the characters and the actors who play them, with Sarah Michelle Gellar, in particular, coming in for detailed criticism or speculation about her face, figure, weight, personality, taste in clothes, alleged affairs with co-stars, marriage to actor Freddie Prinze Jr, alleged rivalry with Alyson Hannigan, interview responses, tattoos, rumoured anorexia and reported cosmetic surgery. Some of the invective directed at the actress is astonishing; not a single area of her life is considered off limits. A journalist friend of mine, who once interviewed her, told me she'd kept referring to herself in the third person – as 'Sarah Michelle Gellar', like a brand name. We both agreed this was creepy and pretentious, though in the light of what I've since read, I can understand why it might be desirable to establish a distance between private self and public persona. Many fans evidently have trouble distinguishing between the actress and the role; they blame Gellar, rather than the writers, for Buffy's behaviour – especially in the later seasons. Some of the more personal comments are reminiscent of the plaints of spurned lovers. You feel relief, on Gellar's behalf, that these people are at home in front of their computers, instead of out on the streets.

So it is that, in Season Six, the nerds come out of the woodwork. Warren, Jonathan and Andrew are sexually and emotionally immature young males whose knowledge of life is second or third-hand, gleaned from superhero comics and role-playing games. They collect merchandising: in 'Smashed', Spike gets them to do his bidding by threatening to damage a figurine of Boba Fett, a minor but ineffably culty character from *Star Wars*. Their concept of villainy is drawn from *Star Wars* and James Bond movies (We're really supervillains now, like Dr No!' crows Andrew) and involves much evil laughter of the sort parodied by the villains in the *Austin Powers* movies. All three dabble in sorcery and robotics (presumably living on the Hellmouth gives them a leg-up in this respect) but their spells have a tendency to go wrong, or have unusual side-effects, or require ingredients that make them snicker like schoolboys ('Stop touching my magic bone!'). Their list of 'Things to Do' includes conjuring fake IDs, developing workable prototype jetpacks and 'girls'. They are in awe of Buffy ('She's hot!') but since the Slayer is the main thing standing between them and their vaguely declared intent to 'take over Sunnydale', she's their designated enemy. There's probably a whiff of sour grapes in there too; Buffy is the epitome of the gorgeous blonde cheerleader type who ignored them at school, and represents all the rejection they've ever felt at the hands of the opposite sex. Now they're out to get their own back. At the very least, they will make her notice them. Which, finally, she does, with the words, 'So you three have ... what? Banded together to be pains in my ass?'

As the most intelligent and bossiest of the three, the leader and spokesman of the Trio is Warren, who was introduced in Season Five; he had a girlfriend, but the fact that he also built a robot love-slave indicates he has a hard time relating to women. The vertically challenged Jonathan has been a familiar face from the very beginning of the series – a recurring background nerd who repeatedly got picked on or shouldered aside. In Season Three, he emerged into the foreground; Buffy talks him out of suicide in 'Earshot' and then, in 'The Prom', it's he who presents her with her Class Protector trophy, one of the few instances when non-Scoobies publicly acknowledge her otherwise unsung heroism (and a sort of in-house Emmy Award for a show whose qualities were consistently overlooked by the prize-giving establishment). In Season Four, Jonathan resurfaces in the alternative Buffyverse episode 'Superstar', which is, one suspects, the only time he ever gets to make out with girls.

The third member of the Trio, Andrew, is almost certainly a virgin, and may well be a closet homosexual, though he's so unworldly he probably wouldn't be aware of it if he were. Nobody remembers or recognises him (naturally enough, since the character isn't introduced until Season Six) though he claims to have once unleashed flying monkey-demons during the Sunnydale High School play (an event we never saw) and in 'The Prom' it was his brother Tucker who trained hellhounds to attack students wearing tuxedos. Andrew is the only one of the Trio who will survive to the end of Season Seven, which features a very funny Andrew-centric episode called 'Storyteller', simultaneously an examination of his nerdy mythomania and a send-up of the series itself. Andrew is the flakiest and most cowardly of the Trio, and also the funniest, though all three are played for laughs until 'Dead Things', when Warren's plan to hypnotise his (by now) ex-girlfriend into becoming his sex-slave ends in her accidental death. Jonathan and Andrew are essentially harmless, but Warren truly intends to kill Buffy, and his deep-rooted feelings of bitterness and resentment towards women, especially women who beat him up in front of his friends, turn him into a catalyst – if not actual force – for evil. Warren's character grows progressively darker until 'Seeing Red', when he triggers the final near-apocalypse – not because he's the Big Bad, but because it's his actions that *create* the Big Bad.

It's here that we're confronted with the consequences of untrammelled nerdism. In Season One, Willow was introduced as the ultimate girl-nerd, and though her blossoming wicca powers, affair with guitarist/werewolf Oz and lesbian relationship with Tara have gone some way to dispelling that first impression, she has never shaken off her nerdlike characteristics – she has always been a little too stuttery, a little too clever at computers, a little too enthusiastic about school or college work. Willow's transformation into a vengeful witch at the end of Season Six has been a long time coming, but her dark side has already been heavily signposted. Her evil vampire id in 'The Wish' (who reappeared in 'Doppelgangland') seemed more comfortable in her own skin than Willow herself.

From the beginning of Season Six and the powerful resurrection spell that brings Buffy back from the dead, Willow has been a little too dependent on magic. When Giles chides her for having messed with dark forces, she replies petulantly, 'I'm very powerful and maybe it's not such a good idea for you to piss me off.' As the season progresses, she relies more and more on magic for trivial things such as tidying her bedroom, like a dark version of Samantha from *Bewitched*, but her spells backfire so frequently it's a wonder she persists with them. In 'All the Way', she casts a spell to make Tara forget a petty argument, but only succeeds in driving her away. In 'Tabula Rasa', another forgetting spell goes wrong, leaving all the main characters with their memories wiped (with hilarious consequences). In 'Smashed', Willow and another witch, Amy (who has just recovered human form after spending three seasons transformed into a rat), amuse themselves by casting humiliating spells on customers at the Bronze, and in 'Wrecked', Amy introduces Willow to the magic equivalent of a crack-den, run by an unsavoury 'dealer' called Rack. Fleeing from a demon conjured by her own magical incontinence, Willow crashes a car, injuring Dawn in the process, after which her friends go into 'intervention' mode to try and stamp out her 'habit'.

All this is a rather heavy-handed analogy of drug and alcohol abuse – something already touched on in the Season Five subplot about Riley's addiction to being bitten by vampires. And, somehow, Willow turning bad doesn't carry the gut-kick impact of Angel turning bad in Season Two. This is partly because news of it was leaked over the Internet long before it happened, and partly because the latter part of the process feels a little rushed. Whereas Angelus got nine episodes – almost half a season – in which to toy sadistically with Buffy's emotions, Willow has a mere three episodes in which to torture and flay Warren, go Terminator on the police station where the other two nerds are being detained, kill Rack, terrorise Dawn (yay!), trash the magic shop and go *mano a mano* with Buffy and Giles before attempting to destroy the world. It's not that we want to see more of *her*; it's just that the other Scoobies' reactions to their friend's transformation seem perfunctory, which is probably inevitable given the limited time.

It's clear from Joss Whedon's DVD commentaries that he has a soft spot, both for Willow and the actress who plays her ('I love Ally in pretty much every scene'[49]). Could it be that, when it came to anointing

Dark Willow: 'Did I have to be so veiny?'

the character as the official Big Bad, he let affection colour his judgment
and postponed her transformation as long as possible?

But he evidently didn't love her enough to allow her to be
beautiful. Like the good-looking vampires who morph into ugly vamp-
face, the witch is disfigured by her wickedness; I have no problem with
her red hair turning black (mine does it all the time, depending on what
dye I've been using) but I'm not so keen on the way her face gets covered
in blue veins. ('Did I have to be so veiny?' laments Hannigan in her DVD
commentary.) Of course it wouldn't do for an evil witch to look too
seductive; it might beam out the wrong sort of message to
impressionable young female audiences, though I have to admit I find
Dark Willow infinitely preferable to the simpering New Agey wicca-
chick of the later seasons, and would like to have seen more of her.
Black magic, murder, playing second fiddle to no man . . . She's almost
worthy of inclusion in the evil sorority of my childhood, alongside
Milady and Maleficient.

Shame about the veins.

9 Sharing the Power

What Happens in Season Seven

All over the world, girls are being stabbed to death by black-robed blind men. The girls are 'Potentials' – Slayers-in-waiting – and the blind men are harbingers of the season's Big Bad, the First Evil, an ancient entity that can assume the likeness of dead people (including Joyce, Warren, Spike, Buffy and earlier Big Bads) who are unable to interact physically with the living, but who goad, torment and trick the other characters throughout the final season.

The new school principal is Robin Wood, who gives Buffy a job as counsellor at the newly rebuilt Sunnydale High. Spike, his soul freshly restored, is back in Sunnydale; at first he's a babbling lunatic hiding in the basement, then the First finds a way to trigger his vampire bloodlust with the Olde English folksong 'Early One Morning' (which his mother used to sing to him), but Buffy's confidence in her ex-lover never wavers. Anya's vengeance demon activities get out of hand; she asks d'Hoffryn, her demon boss, to put her out of her misery, but instead of killing her he makes her mortal. Willow returns from convalescing in Giles's English country mansion, but is nervous about using magic again. Xander provides solid emotional support and not much else. Dawn continues to be annoying.

Andrew and Jonathan return to Sunnydale; under the influence of the First, Andrew kills Jonathan in an abortive attempt to open the

Hellmouth, situated directly beneath Principal Wood's office; it's later opened with Spike's blood, and disgorges a particularly powerful and dangerous übervampire which Buffy defeats only with the greatest difficulty. She later has a vision in which she sees the Hellmouth swarming with such creatures. Andrew is detained by the Scoobies and made to see the error of his ways, though he continues to get on everybody's nerves with his nerdy wittering. Meanwhile, frightened Potentials from all around the world are seeking refuge in Sunnydale and lodging at the Summers house, which begins to resemble a girls' dormitory; Buffy tries to mould them into a fighting team, but is hampered by low morale and lack of information about the enemy.

Willow forms an intimate bond with Kennedy, one of the Potentials. The First destroys the London HQ of the Watchers' Council, killing all the Watchers apart from Giles, who hotfoots it back to Sunnydale. Principal Wood turns out to be the son of the Slayer killed by Spike in New York in 1977, but Wood's bid for revenge on the vampire fails, and he and Giles (who distracted the Slayer while this was going on) only succeed in antagonising Buffy. The Hellmouth is exercising an unusually bad influence on the Sunnydale High students and the local police. The townsfolk, sensing the end is nigh, are starting to pack up and leave.

123

Principal Wood: son of Nikki the Vampire Slayer

Caleb, an evil preacher and earthly representative of the First, sets up shop in a nearby vineyard, where he kicks Buffy's ass, kills a couple of Potentials and puts out one of Xander's eyes. Afterwards, there's friction at the Summers house; Dawn, the Scoobies and the Potentials gang up against Buffy, who is driven out of her own home. Faith, who has come back to Sunnydale a reformed character (she escaped from prison in Los Angeles after attempts were made on her life), is persuaded to take charge, but Caleb lures her into a trap in which several Potentials are killed. Buffy comes perilously close to giving up, but continues to have a staunch ally in Spike. Invigorated by his pep talk, she outwits Caleb and finds a mystical scythe with which she slices the evil preacher in half. Angel pops up to present her with a mystical amulet; Buffy is pleased to see him but sends him back to Los Angeles and gives the amulet to Spike.

On the eve of the big showdown, Faith and Principal Wood have sex. Willow and Kennedy have sex. Anya and Xander have sex. Buffy and Spike spend the night together, though it's not clear as to whether or not they too have sex. Buffy comes up with a daring plan: she will turn her back on the tradition of the solitary Slayer and share her power with the other Potentials. Willow casts the sharing spell just

Caleb the evil preacher

One-eyed Xander

in time for the big fight against zillions of übervamps in the basement of
Sunnydale High. The battle is hard and long. Anya and some of the
Potentials die, but with the help of the mystical scythe, shared Slayer
power and Spike, who sacrifices himself, the forces of evil are finally
routed. Buffy, Dawn, the Scoobies, Principal Wood, Faith and the
surviving Potentials make it out of Sunnydale on the old school bus just
as the town collapses into the Hellmouth, leaving an enormous crater.
Giles announces there's another Hellmouth in Cleveland . . .

125

Joss Whedon said,

> I designed Buffy to be an icon, to be an emotional experience, to be
> loved in a way that other shows can't be loved. Because it's about
> adolescence, which is the most important thing people go through in
> their development, becoming an adult. And it mythologizes it in such a
> way, such a romantic way – it basically says, 'Everybody who made it
> through adolescence is a hero'.[50]

But in bringing Buffy's story to a satisfying conclusion, the seventh and
final season flies even further in the face of heroic tradition than Season

Six. In the final episode, Buffy isn't just rejecting the rules made up by 'a bunch of men . . . hundreds of years ago' when she decides to share her power: 'I say my power will be *our* power.' She's also rebelling against the manifesto of the very series of which she is the heroine: 'In every generation there is a Chosen One. She alone will stand against the vampires, the demons and the forces of darkness.' She is blowing apart the confines of her own fiction.

This is a glorious, positive and impeccably moral conclusion – and a hard-won one. At times, Season Seven makes uncomfortable viewing as Buffy becomes increasingly isolated from family and friends – even more so than in Season Six – and is forced to confront what being a hero really means. There has always been an implicit ethical problem with superheroes – just because they have superpowers, does that mean they're better than the rest of us? Superman, Spider-Man and their ilk, of course, were good guys, but as 'with great power comes great responsibility', so there's always the potential for mighty heroes to use their power for evil instead of good, just as German Fascists twisted the Niebelungen myths to fit their own perverted ideology. Like Faith, Jean Grey or Anakin Skywalker, any superhero can embrace the Dark Side and turn into a rogue Slayer, Dark Phoenix or Darth Vader. Being super, as Anya tells Buffy, 'doesn't make you better than us – it makes you

The Potentials: Slayers-in-waiting

luckier than us.' It's doubtful that Buffy feels lucky, though, since in Season Seven, more than ever before, the weight of the world is on her shoulders: family and friends repeatedly let her down, fail to watch her back or appreciate what she's going through, and she's forced to wrestle with her own superiority complex, worrying that even though her friends love her, 'it doesn't mean anything because their opinions don't matter,' and declaring, 'Democracies don't win battles', before a shattering last-minute crisis, when her attempt to assert her leadership and make unpopular decisions after the first catastrophic confrontation with Caleb ends with Willow, Xander, Giles and Dawn, as well as the Potentials, turning against her and driving her out of her own home.

After six seasons of being supported by the Scooby Gang, Buffy finally has to go it alone and reassert her individuality. In Season Seven, she helps and protects Spike when everyone else insists he's not to be trusted, remains true to her beliefs even when they're unpopular and refuses to back down and play nice when everyone gangs up against her. When she's cast out of her own house (which I think is a bit rich; I mean, is it *Dawn* who pays the bills?), she finds herself as much of an outsider as she was when she first arrived in Sunnydale (maybe more so, because her mother's no longer there to back her up), and when Faith's leadership ends in disaster and Buffy regains her position at the head of the group, she's all the stronger for having been forced, however temporarily, to take stock of the situation from an outsider's point of view. The Potentials are quick to blame Faith for leading them into a trap, but Buffy admits, 'That could have just as easily happened to me.' Symptomatically, while friends and family are ganging up on her, it's only erstwhile enemies Spike and Faith who understand her plight and show her any sympathy, and Faith isn't sorry to hand the reins back to Buffy: 'Everyone's looking to me, trusting me to lead them, and I've never felt so alone in my entire life ... And that's you every day, isn't it?'

The modus operandi of the season's Big Bad, the ultimate evil known as the First (encountered as early as Season Three, when it announced, 'I am the thing that darkness fears' and tormented Angel in the guise of three of his victims, including Jenny Calendar), is to adopt the likenesses of dead people, one of whom is Buffy herself (she died twice, remember?). It's a neat bit of symbolism, in that Buffy's own worst enemy is . . . Buffy! Though the First is briefly glimpsed as a huge horned CGI demon pouring its essence into Caleb, it's more formidable – and far sneakier – when approaching the characters in the guise of their loved ones (Principal Wood's mother, or Faith's surrogate father Mayor Wilkins) to whisper unpalatable truths into their ears, applying pressure to their weak spots – Willow's fear that if she uses magic again she will lose control, for example. Throughout the series, the villains have shown a knack for telling it like it is while the heroes have been blinded by their emotions: in Season Three, both Spike and the Mayor inform Buffy and Angel there's no future in their relationship even before they've realised it themselves. But it's this hurtful truth-telling that turns out to be the Big Bad's Achilles heel in Season Seven, since the first step to overcoming our flaws is to realise what they are. Buffy's evil likeness, her negative alter ego, taunts her with what it knows is the chink in her armour, repeatedly reminding her of the loneliness of the long-distance Slayer and the sense of isolation that has alienated her from her friends. But all this harping on the word 'alone' only succeeds in eventually tipping her off as to what she must do. In order *not* to be alone, she must share her superpowers, her responsibilities, her role as the one true Slayer.

She's not the first hero to understand the need to share the power. The Seven Samurai didn't stand alone against the rampaging bandits; they taught the villagers how to fight alongside them. Howard Hawks directed *Rio Bravo* (1959) as a riposte to the hero-standing-alone plot of *High Noon* (1952), surrounding *his* sheriff with a motley bunch of allies. In *The Outlaw Josey Wales* (1976), it's Josey's surrogate family that helps him overcome his destructive lust for revenge. These characters are the opposite of those in the films of, say, Michael Mann: in *Thief* (1981), Frank decides he has to go it alone if he's going to survive as a superthief, while Neil McCauley in *Heat* (1995) echoes his philosophy, 'A guy told me one time, "Don't let yourself get attached to anything you are not willing to walk out on in thirty seconds flat if you

Buffy the Vampire Slayer in action

feel the heat around the corner." ' In fact, Buffy's approach flies in the face of Hollywood tradition, in which the West is won thanks to lone gunslingers, hero cops are go-it-alone mavericks, partners invariably turn out to be betrayers or cannon fodder – and female characters are little more than decorative bystanders.

129

Throughout seven seasons, but especially during the final two, Buffy has had to struggle not to let her superior strength pervert her humanity. She makes mistakes, has to wrestle with her own shortcomings, but her ultimate choices have always been the right ones. Her punning last words to that pesky doppelgänger, who turns up one last time to sneer at her during the final battle, are, 'I want you to get out of my face!' She has struggled against her own worst impulses – and won.

From El Cid to William Wallace to Davy Crockett, we are accustomed to heroes sacrificing themselves for their cause. Buffy has already proved, more than once, that she's willing to go the whole nine yards, and the build-up to the end of Season Seven leads us to expect a worst-case scenario by piling on the mood of gathering storm, with our heroine remarking gloomily every half-hour or so that, 'This isn't some story where Good triumphs,' or, 'Not all of us are going to make it.' Even though we know perfectly well that Good *will* ultimately triumph (this is prime-time TV, for heaven's sake, not some nihilistic 1970s conspiracy thriller), as the series rolls towards its close there is an oppressive, almost depressing sense of destiny creeping up and nipping at the heels of the regular characters. Not everyone is going to make it out of here alive, that much is clear. But who will be sacrificed? Xander or Willow? Giles? Faith? Principal Wood? Or (please, please) Dawn? Is Buffy herself going to make it a hat-trick? Is *everyone* going to die?

For all the First's sneakiness, its amorphous incorporeality isn't much cop in a *mano a mano* situation, so when it comes to the crunch it's forced to delegate clobbering duties to hordes of strong but not terribly bright übervampire minions who all of a sudden seem less invincible than in previous episodes (and who look and behave more like *Lord of the Rings*-style Orcs than vampires anyway). In the end, although several Potentials and about a zillion übervampires bite the dust in the final showdown, the only casualties among our regular characters are the two demons. Or, in Anya's case, ex-demon, as she finally learns what it means to be mortal, a fate already foreshadowed in 'Selfless' (an episode featuring some droll subtitled flashbacks to her origins in mediaeval Sjornjost) when she berates her demon boss, d'Hoffryn, for not killing her as she requested, and he replies ominously, 'All good things come in time.' After her vengeance demon recidivism in the same episode (she summons a spider-demon to rip the hearts out of a houseful of frat boys), Buffy resolves to kill her with an alarming lack of soul-searching and a rapidity that was notably absent from her tolerant, forgiving attitude towards similarly murderous behaviour from her best buddy Willow or her vampire boyfriends.

Anya survives Buffy's swordthrust on that occasion, but goes on to pay the price in the final showdown when in a fleeting but nonetheless shocking image we see her sliced down the middle by an übervamp blade. Some fans, presumably more accustomed to long and maudlin TV death scenes, were outraged that her demise was so abrupt ('I will never forgive them for Anya's death. Blink and you'd have missed it'[51]) and were even more discountenanced by Xander's reaction when informed that his ex had died saving Andrew: 'That's my girl, always doing the stupid thing.'

Spike makes the ultimate sacrifice

('He should have been more upset.')[52] In fact, Xander's attempt at
flippancy is more moving than any amount of bereaved sobbing, and
Nicholas Brendon's hint of a lip-tremble gives the moment more poignant
clout than any amount of wailing and breast-beating would have done.
This was conscious policy on Whedon's part; Anthony Stewart Head,
who as Giles had been advised to react to the death of Jenny Calendar in a
similarly understated way, quotes him as saying, 'As soon as you cry, you
rob the audience of being able to cry themselves.'[53]

    The other big casualty is Spike, who completes his six-season
character arc from vampire villain to vampire hero, and dies laughing as
the mystic amulet around his neck turns into a sort of flashing disco
medallion and unleashes giant laser beams of sunshine to dust all the
vampires (himself included) in the vicinity – though the magnanimity of
this gesture is slightly diminished by the foreknowledge that he will
shortly be resurrected as a regular in Season Five of *Angel*.

    Where Anya's death is sudden and shocking, Spike's is more
prolonged, allowing time for he and Buffy to exchange meaningful
glances and for her to squeeze out the words 'I love you' before she is

131

forced to run for her life, leaving her spontaneously combusting ex-lover to mop up the evil dregs. Mercifully, Whedon knows how to deflate the statement's mawkishness, and at the same time make it all the more touching, by having Spike reply, 'No you don't, but thanks for saying it.' That's our boy, straight-shooter to the last.

Poor Spike and Anya. Their reward for being the rebels, individualists and most interesting characters in Seasons Six and Seven is death. And part of the reason they have been the most interesting characters, with the most compelling story arcs, is that they have taken the place of Buffy, Willow and Xander as outsiders and identity figures. Buffy, Xander and Willow – and to a lesser extent Giles – who started out in Season One as *personae non grata* in Sunnydale's trendiest circles, have been knotted by five seasons of supernatural adversity into the sort of smug little clique from which they themselves might once have been excluded. Despite Spike and Anya's attempts to shed their demonic natures and forge lasting emotional relationships with humans, despite fighting shoulder to shoulder with the other Scoobies, despite all their hard work and loyalty, it's only in death that they can be accepted as part of the core group. Partly, of course, this is because they are both ex-demons who must atone for centuries of bad behaviour, but partly because it's only by dying that they can prove beyond contention their willingness to embrace the human condition – a Catch-22 situation if ever there was one.

So, RIP Spike and Anya, who don't even get the compensation of a 'They saved the world' tombstone. Nevertheless, I can't help feeling the final body count isn't big enough. Maybe it's simple bloodthirstiness on my part, but in terms of reaping-what-you-sow, I reckon some of the other characters get off lightly. Willow's reward for turning evil, flaying Warren, killing Rack (OK, so he was a sleazy piece of work, but we've seen worse in this series), trying to kill her friends and attempting to destroy the world turns out to be comfy convalescence in an English country house, followed by a warm welcome back into the bosom of Sunnydale, an attractive new girlfriend (Kennedy, who despite her pierced tongue never got on my nerves the way Tara did) and newly enhanced wicca powers; we should all be so lucky. All right, so she feels guilty, but as a slap on the wrist this doesn't begin to compare with, say, Angel's lengthy sojourn in a hell dimension between Seasons Two and Three.

When he gets skewered in the final showdown, it looks for a while as though Principal Wood might pay the ultimate price for his ill-judged attempt to kill Spike, but he survives his wound to exchange a flirtatious quip with Faith. Faith's own history of murder and torture might have made the death penalty a fitting retribution, but the time she has served in prison is evidently deemed punishment enough (and Whedon might have wanted to keep open the option for a Faith-centric spin-off series). Andrew, after killing his friend Jonathan (albeit under the First's influence – but to what extent is this a mitigating circumstance?) was surely a candidate for the chop but survives intact, much to his own surprise. Personally, I would have liked to see Dawn getting it in the neck after her three seasons of whining and squealing; I can understand how her death would possibly have been construed as gratuitous and unreasonable, but surely a couple of flesh-wounds might not have gone amiss? After all, poor old Xander loses an eye. Then again, he never did atone for having caused the deaths of several townsfolk by conjuring the song-and-dance demon in 'Once More, with Feeling'. As for Giles, I don't seem to remember him paying for having killed Ben at the end of Season Five; admittedly, in doing so he was also destroying Glory, but it wasn't poor Ben's fault he was sharing physical space with the Big Bad.

But while more fatalities and/or loss of important body parts might have added more of an emotional punch to the finale and left us feeling weepier, Whedon was understandably reluctant to bump off his main human characters – 'I couldn't kill any of my Core Four and still call it a happy ending'.[54] Buffy, Giles, Willow and Xander survive with only the loss of an eye between them, and are last seen standing on the edge of the crater ('like John Steinbeck characters'[55]) where Sunnydale used to stand. In the end, good or bad behaviour doesn't really enter into it; the only foolproof way to stay alive is to be one of the creator's

133

The last battle

favourites – preferably one of the Core Four. And because these characters have spent the last seven years entertaining us, because we've laughed and suffered with them, because they've surprised and delighted and annoyed us, we've almost come to think of them as real people, as real friends, and, since they're friends, we're prepared to let them get away with murder. As you do.

We're all members of the Scooby Gang now.

For me, though, the highlight of the last episode is that Bosch-like vision of Buffy, Faith and the other Potentials on the brink of the Hellmouth, hacking and slicing and kicking their way through wave after wave of übervamps. Even now I can't listen to Robert Duncan's stirring 'Last Battle' music without tears welling up in my eyes. It's a majestic swirling theme with a touch of Conan and a dash of Celtic (evoking big-scale kilt epics such as *Braveheart* [1995] and, to a lesser extent, *Highlander*) and the final, incontrovertible proof that my female action heroine is up there on screen, at last. She's made it. My beautiful vampire killer, with her long hair and pretty clothes, with all her doubts and fears, her courage and fortitude and silliness and girly-fu, has finally smashed the genre rulebook, trampled all over tradition and assumed her rightful place in the pantheon of pop culture.

10 After *Buffy*

Angel, the series, continued to explore the Buffyverse for another year until it was abruptly cancelled by the network. Whedon and his co-pilot David Greenwalt ensured the series went out with an apocalyptic bang, though not before Buffy, Willow, Spike, Harmony, Andrew and (when Sarah Michelle Gellar proved unavailable) the back of Buffy's head had all made appearances in the course of its five seasons.

But the Slayer's fame has spread far and wide, beyond the confines of nerd-dom and the cult TV crowd. Though they might not have watched a single episode, parents and teachers, politicians and academics have all heard of her; that silly name paid off, after all – it's hard to imagine that a vampire slayer called Joan or Mary would have lodged in the collective consciousness the same way. Buffy now pops up in the strangest places: in a paper titled 'Biological Warfare and the Buffy Paradigm', Anthony Cordesman, a military analyst and holder of the Arleigh A. Burke Chair in Strategy at the Center for Strategic and International Studies, maintained that the problems faced by Buffy and her friends are not unlike the challenges faced by the United States in the war against terrorism.[56]

And, just as *Buffy the Vampire Slayer* picked and mixed elements from older films and TV shows, so more recent TV series continue to borrow elements from *Buffy the Vampire Slayer*. Led by *Xena: Warrior Princess* (1995–2001), action heroines leapt, kicked and swung swords in *Highlander: The Raven* (1989–99), *Dark Angel* (2000–2), *La Femme Nikita* (1997–2001) and *Witchblade* (2001–2). Pretty young women cast magic spells in *Charmed* (1998–?) and *Hex* (2004), conversed with God in *Joan of Arcadia* (2003–5), played the Grim Reaper in *Dead Like Me* (2003–4), listened to model animals in

Wonderfalls (2004), wrestled with a diabolical heritage in *Point Pleasant* (2005), solved crimes with many a Buffy-like quip in *Veronica Mars* (2004–?), solved crimes the psychic way in *Medium* (2005), empathised with serial killers in *The Inside* (2005) and listened to corpses in *Tru Calling* (2003–4), which starred Eliza Dushku, better known in the Buffyverse as Faith. High-school students flexed superhuman muscle in *Roswell* (1999–2002), *Smallville* (2001–) and *Vampire High* (2001).

In many of these shows, there's a marked attempt to marry the supernatural or paranormal aspects with the heroine's domestic or private life, though most of the shows were also founded on inflexible gimmicks (concepts that might have formed the basis of a single episode, at most, of *Buffy the Vampire Slayer*) and failed to last the course. The most successful post-Buffy heroine is probably Sydney in *Alias*, a smart espionage fantasy variation modelled on the tried and tested format: Adventure-of-the-Week hitched to long-term story arc, kick-ass action scenes, girly clothes (and wigs, lots of wigs) and an almost transcendentally complicated emotional life.

The *Buffy* effect is less apparent in film, though teen movies such as *10 Things I Hate about You* (1999) and *Bring It On* (2000) continue to show traces of intelligent life, while a flood of paranormal high-school movies from Japan and Korea (*Whasango/Volcano High* [2002], *Uzumaki* [2000], *Eko Eko Azaraku/Wizard of Darkness* [1995], *Yeogo Goedam/Whispering Corridors* [1998] and so forth) have found a readymade western audience in the legions of *Buffy* fans searching for surrogates to replace their favourite show.

Rumoured *Buffy the Vampire Slayer* spin-offs featuring Ripper (aka Giles), Faith and Spike, as well as *Buffy the Vampire Slayer – The Animated Series*, have yet to see the light of day. Joss Whedon's sci-fi-cum-Western TV series, *Firefly* (2002), barely made it out of the starting gate before being axed by the big bad network (several of the regular cast found their way onto later episodes of *Buffy the Vampire Slayer* or *Angel*), but built up a strong following on DVD and formed the basis of Whedon's feature film-directing debut, *Serenity* (2005). Buffy's creator, who obviously finds that masterminding, writing or

Fray the future slayer

directing a clutch of TV shows and movies leaves him with way too
much time on his hands (no wonder he failed to see why Maggie Walsh
shouldn't teach psychology and run a complex covert paramilitary
operation at the same time), has also dipped his toe into the world of
graphic novels. *Fray* (2003) extends the Buffyverse forward several
centuries into the future, with superthief Melaka Fray inheriting the
Slayer scythe. Whedon also found time to write stories for *Tales of the
Slayers* (2001) and *Tales of the Vampires* (2004) – collections of graphic
novellas describing past, present and future incidents in the lives and
deaths of the Slayers, their Watchers and their foes – as well as to pay
direct tribute to Kitty Pryde, Buffy's forebear, in a new *X-Men* series,
Astonishing X-Men (2004–?). Whedon was at one time slated to write
and direct the third *X-Men* movie, but instead signed on to write and
direct a new movie about Wonder Woman, whom he declares 'the most
iconic female heroine of our time', saying, 'What I love most about icons
is finding out what's behind them, exploring the price of their power.'[57]

    Buffy's comic-strip career doesn't stop there. The Buffyverse
lives on in dozens of *Buffy the Vampire Slayer* and *Angel* graphic novels
that fill the gaps between episodes or seasons; here you can discover
what happened to Pike, Buffy's romantic interest in the 1992 film, or
follow the Scoobies' adventures prior to Buffy's resurrection, or roll
your eyes at Dawn's alternative version of highlights (presumably

137

programmed into her memory by monks) from Seasons One to Four. Needless to say, the character is every bit as irritating in graphic novel form as she was in the TV series.

Meanwhile, the *Buffy* industry continues to produce a never-ending stream of merchandise: graphic novels, calendars and diaries, novels, dictionaries and guides to *Buffy*-related philosophy, theology and gender studies. There are CDs and DVDs, action figures and busts (even minor demons such as d'Hoffryn and Kulak are commemorated in hand-painted porcelain), masks, trading cards, games, mugs and posters, lollipops and lunch boxes, alarm clocks and keychains, pencil cases and Welcome to the Hellmouth Do-Not-Disturb signs. This is par for the course for cult films and TV shows, of course, but the difference with the Buffyverse, which can hold its own against *Star Wars*, *The Lord of the Rings*, *The Matrix*, *Star Trek* or *Harry Potter*, is that this is the first time such a cult has built up around a *girl*.

Buffy beat out Lara Croft, heroine of the 1996 computer game 'Tomb Raider', to become the first Female Internet Superstar with universal appeal, and *Buffy the Vampire Slayer*, the series, was in the vanguard of a burgeoning trend for discussing and dissecting TV shows in online chatrooms and forums, which have replaced the office 'water cooler' as a place where fans can gather to talk about last night's must-see television. The Internet has restored a sense of community, however virtual, to audiences long since split asunder by the proliferation and divergence of television into a million different cable and satellite channels, but *Buffy*, in particular, has bridged genders, geographical distances and generation gaps in a way no television show has done before.

It took fifty years of television, but I finally found the action heroine of my dreams. And while Buffy may have reached the end of her journey, her legacy lives on. Wherever there are vampires to be slain, high schools to be endured or small girls searching for role models, Buffy will be there. Thanks to her, we can never again be sure that 'the little blonde girl who goes into a dark alley' is fated to be just another victim. Maybe, sometimes, she's going to turn around and kick ass.

Television will never be the same again.

Appendix: My Favourite Episodes

'The Puppet Show' – the one with Sophocles over the end credits

'Innocence' – Angel turns back into Angelus and is beastly to Buffy

'Passion' – Angelus kills Jenny, Giles reacts

'The Wish' – alternative Sunnydale

'Earshot' – Buffy reads minds

'The Prom' – Buffy breaks up with Angel, but saves the prom; the other students present her with a symbol of their appreciation

'Hush' – the Gentlemen come to town

'Restless' – the dream episode

'Fool for Love' – Spike's flashbacks

'Once More, with Feeling' – the musical episode

'Selfless' – flashbacks to Anya's pre-demon past in Scandinavia, with subtitles

'Conversations with Dead People' – Buffy gets psychoanalysed by a vampire

'Storyteller' – Andrew films the Scoobies

'Chosen' – the Last Battle

Notes

1 Andrea Weiss, *Vampires and Violets: Lesbians in Film* (New York: Penguin, 1993).

2 Carol J. Clover, *Men, Women and Chainsaws: Gender in the Modern Horror Film* (London: BFI, 1992).

3 Joss Whedon, DVD commentary on 'Welcome to the Hellmouth'.

4 Whedon interview, <www.theonionavclub.com>.

5 <www.slayage.tv/discoveringbuffy/discoveringbuffy_g-k.htm>.

6 Whedon, DVD commentary on 'Welcome to the Hellmouth'.

7 Ibid.

8 Ibid.

9 Ibid.

10 Ibid.

11 Ibid.

12 <www.christiananswers.net>.

13 <www.parentstv.org/PTC/publications/reports/top10bestandworst/2002/top10worst.asp>.

14 Michael Adams, *Slayer Slang: A Buffy the Vampire Slayer Lexicon* (New York: Oxford University Press, 2003).

15 Whedon interview, <www.theonionavclub. com>.

16 Whedon, DVD commentary on 'Innocence'.

17 <www.post-gazette.com/tv/200107 17owen0717p3.asp>.

18 Whedon, DVD commentary on 'Welcome to the Hellmouth'.

19 Ibid.

20 Ibid.

21 Whedon, DVD commentary on 'Innocence'.

22 Ibid.

23 Ibid.

24 Ibid.

25 Ibid.

26 Ibid.

27 Whedon interview, <www.theonionavclub.com>.

28 Whedon, DVD commentary on 'Welcome to the Hellmouth'.

29 <www.thecityofabsurdity.com>.

30 Whedon, 'Season Three overview', DVD mini-feature.

31 Sigourney Weaver interviewed by the author, 'Alien Nation', *GQ* (UK), 1992.

32 Whedon interviewed for MSN, 'In Joss We Trust . . .', <entertainment.msn.com/news/article.aspx?news=122421&mpc=2>.

33 Whedon interviewed in *In Focus* magazine, <www.infocusmag.com/05augustseptember/whedonuncut.htm>.

34 Interview with Jane Espenson, in Nancy Holder *et al.*, *The Watcher's Guide Volume 2* (New York: Pocket Books, 2000).

35 'In Joss We Trust . . .'.

36 Script available as DVD extra to 'Hush'.

37 Whedon, DVD commentary on 'Hush'.

38 Whedon, DVD commentary on 'Restless'.

39 Ibid.

40 Ibid.

41 Ibid.

42 David Fury and James A. Contner, DVD commentary on 'Primeval'.

43 Whedon, DVD commentary on 'The Body'.

44 Mark Armstrong, 'UPN Smacks down Bid for *Buffy*', <www.fansite.com/News/Items/PF/0,1527,8002,00.html>.

45 <www.aintitcool.com>.

46 Whedon interview, <www.theonionavclub. com>.

47 Jonathan Green, *The Cassell Dictionary of Slang* (London: Cassell, 1998).

48 Heir to Shadow, 'Educating Buffy', <www.vampirecows.com/odd/authors/heir/educatingbuffybg.html>.

49 Whedon, DVD commentary on 'Chosen'.

50 Whedon interview, <www.theonionavclub.com>.

51 Fiona, <community.channel4.com/groupee/forums/a/tpc>.

52 Ibid.

53 <actionadventure.about.com/library/weekly/2002/aa051502.htm>.

54 Whedon, DVD commentary on 'Chosen'.

55 Ibid.

56 Lisa Tozzi, 'Slaying Terrorism, It's Good to Be Buffy', *New York Times*, 4 August 2002.

57 <film.guardian.co.uk/news/story/0,12589,1444817,00.html>.

Credits

Buffy the Vampire Slayer

Created by Joss Whedon
Executive producers: Sandy
Gallin, Gail Berman, Fran
Rubel Kuzui, Kaz Kuzui

Production companies:
Mutant Enemy, Inc./Kuzui
Enterprises/Sandollar
Television

SEASON ONE – *main cast*
Sarah Michelle Gellar (Buffy
Summers). Nicholas Brendon
(Xander Harris). Alyson
Hannigan (Willow
Rosenberg). Charisma
Carpenter (Cordelia Chase).
Anthony Stewart Head
(Rupert Giles).
©1997.
[Witch episode ©1996.
Twentieth Century Fox Film
Corporation]

**10/3/1997 Welcome to the
Hellmouth**
dir. Charles Martin Smith,
wr. Joss Whedon
Guest cast: Mark Metcalf,
Brian Thompson, David
Boreanaz, Ken Lerner,
Kristine Sutherland, Julie
Benz, J. Patrick Lawlor, Eric
Balfour
10/3/1997 The Harvest
dir. John T. Kretchmer,
wr. Joss Whedon
Guest cast: Mark Metcalf,
Brian Thompson, David
Boreanaz, Ken Lerner,
Kristine Sutherland, Julie
Benz, Eric Balfour
17/3/1997 Witch
dir. Stephen Cragg,
wr. Dana Reston
Guest cast: Kristine
Sutherland, Elizabeth Anne
Allen, Robin Riker

24/3/1997 Teacher's Pet
dir. Bruce Seth Green,
wr. David Greenwalt
Guest cast: David Boreanaz,
Ken Lerner, Musetta Vander,
Jackson Price, Jean Speegle
Howard
31/3/1997 Never Kill a Boy
on the First Date
dir. David Semel, wr. Rob Des
Hotel, Dean Batali
Guest cast: Mark Metcalf,
David Boreanaz, Christopher
Wiehl, Geoff Meed
7/4/1997 The Pack
dir. Bruce Seth Green, wr.
Matt Kiene, Joe Reinkemeyer
Guest cast: Ken Lerner, Eion
Bailey, Michael McRaine,
Brian Gross, Jennifer Sky, Jeff
Maynard, James Stephens
14/4/1997 Angel
dir. Scott Brazil, wr. David
Greenwalt
Guest cast: Mark Metcalf,
David Boreanaz, Kristine
Sutherland, Julie Benz
**28/4/1997 I Robot . . . You
Jane**
dir. Stephen Posey, wr. Ashley
Gable, Thomas A. Swyden
Guest cast: Robia La Morte,
Chad Lindberg, Jamison Ryan
5/5/1997 The Puppet Show
dir. Ellen S. Pressman, wr.
Dean Batali, Rob Des Hotel
Guest cast: Kristine
Sutherland, Richard Werner,
Burke Roberts, Armin
Shimerman
12/5/1997 Nightmares
dir. Bruce Seth Green,
teleplay: David Greenwalt,
story: Joss Whedon
Guest cast: Mark Metcalf,
Kristine Sutherland, Jeremy
Foley, Andrew J. Ferchland
**19/5/1997 Out of Mind, Out
of Sight**
dir. Reza Badiyi, teleplay:
Ashley Gable, Thomas A.

Swyden, story: Joss Whedon
Guest cast: David Boreanaz,
Clea DuVall, Armin
Shimerman
2/6/1997 Prophecy Girl
dir./wr. Joss Whedon
Guest cast: Mark Metcalf,
David Boreanaz, Kristine
Sutherland, Robia La Morte,
Andrew J. Ferchland

SEASON TWO – *main cast*
Sarah Michelle Gellar (Buffy
Summers). Nicholas Brendon
(Xander Harris). Alyson
Hannigan (Willow Rosenberg).
Charisma Carpenter (Cordelia
Chase). David Boreanaz
(Angel). Anthony Stewart
Head (Rupert Giles).
©1997/1998.

**15/9/1997 When She Was
Bad**
dir./wr. Joss Whedon
Guest cast: Kristine
Sutherland, Robia La Morte,
Andrew J. Ferchland, Dean
Butler, Brent Jennings, Armin
Shimerman
**22/9/1997 Some Assembly
Required**
dir. Bruce Seth Green, wr. Ty
King
Guest cast: Robia La Morte,
Angelo Spizzirri, Michael
Bacall, Ingo Neuhaus,
Melanie MacQueen
29/9/1997 School Hard
dir. John T. Kretchmer,
teleplay: David Greenwalt,
story: Joss Whedon, David
Greenwalt
Guest cast: Kristine
Sutherland, Robia La Morte,
Andrew J. Ferchland, James
Marsters, Alexandra Johnes,
Gregory Scott Cummins,
Andrew Palmer, Brian Reddy,
Juliet Landau, Armin
Shimerman

6/10/1997 Inca Mummy Girl
dir. Ellen S. Pressman, wr.
Matt Kiene, Joe Reinkemeyer
Guest cast: Kristine
Sutherland, Ara Celi, Seth
Green
13/10/1997 Reptile Boy
dir./wr. David Greenwalt
Guest cast: Greg Vaughn,
Todd Babcock, Jordana Spiro
27/10/1997 Halloween
dir. Bruce Seth Green, wr.
Carl Ellsworth
Guest cast: Seth Green,
James Marsters, Robin Sachs,
Juliet Landau, Armin
Shimerman
3/11/1997 Lie to Me
dir./wr. Joss Whedon
Guest cast: Robia La Morte,
James Marsters, Jason Behr,
Jarrad Paul, Juliet Landau
10/11/1997 The Dark Age
dir. Bruce Seth Green, wr.
Dean Batali, Rob Des Hotel
Guest cast: Robia La Morte,
Robin Sachs, Stuart McLean
**17/11/1997 What's My Line?,
part one**
dir. David Solomon, wr.
Howard Gordon, Marti Noxon
Guest cast: Seth Green,
James Marsters, Eric Saiet,
Kelly Connell, Bianca
Lawson, Saverio Guerra,
Juliet Landau, Armin
Shimerman
**24/11/1997 What's My Line?,
part two**
dir. David Semel, wr. Marti
Noxon
Guest cast: Seth Green,
Saverio Guerra, Kelly Connell,
Bianca Lawson, James
Marsters, Juliet Landau
8/12/1997 Ted
dir. Bruce Seth Green, wr.
David Greenwalt, Joss Whedon
Guest cast: John Ritter,
Kristine Sutherland, Robia La
Morte, Ken Thorley, James G.
MacDonald
12/1/1998 Bad Eggs
dir. David Greenwalt, wr.
Marti Noxon

Guest cast: Kristine
Sutherland, Jeremy
Ratchford, James Parks,
Rick Zieff
19/1/1998 Surprise
dir. Michael Lange, wr. Marti
Noxon
Guest cast: Seth Green,
Kristine Sutherland, Robia La
Morte, Brian Thompson, Ryan
Francis, Vincent Schiavelli,
James Marsters
20/1/1998 Innocence
dir./wr. Joss Whedon
Guest cast: Seth Green,
Kristine Sutherland, Robia La
Morte, Brian Thompson, Eric
Saiet, Vincent Schiavelli,
James Marsters, Juliet
Landau
27/1/1998 Phases
dir. Bruce Seth Green, wr.
Rob Des Hotel, Dean Batali
Guest cast: Seth Green,
Camila Griggs, Jack Conley
**10/2/1998 Bewitched,
Bothered and Bewildered**
dir. James A. Contner, wr.
Marti Noxon
Guest cast: Seth Green,
Kristine Sutherland, Robia La
Morte, Elizabeth Anne Allen,
Mercedes McNab, Lorna
Scott, James Marsters, Juliet
Landau
24/2/1998 Passion
dir. Michael E. Gershman, wr.
Ty King
Guest cast: Kristine
Sutherland, Robia La Morte,
Richard Assad, James
Marsters, Juliet Landau
3/3/1998 Killed by Death
dir. Deran Serafian, wr. Rob
Des Hotel, Dean Batali
Guest cast: Kristine
Sutherland, Richard Herd,
Willie Garson, Andrew
Ducote, Juanita Jennings
**28/4/1998 I Only Have Eyes
for You**
dir. James Whitmore, Jr., wr.
Marti Noxon
Guest cast: Meredith
Salinger, Christopher Gorham,

John Hawkes, Miriam Flynn,
Brian Reddy, James Marsters,
Juliet Landau, Armin
Shimerman
5/5/1998 Go Fish
dir. David Semel, wr. David
Fury, Elin Hampton
Guest cast: Charles Cyphers,
Jeremy Garrett, Wentworth
Miller, Conchata Ferrell,
Armin Shimerman
**12/5/1998 Becoming,
part one**
dir./wr. Joss Whedon
Guest cast: Max Perlich, Seth
Green, Kristine Sutherland,
Julie Benz, Bianca Lawson,
Jack McGee, Richard Riehle,
James Marsters, Juliet
Landau, Armin Shimerman
**19/5/1998 Becoming,
part two**
dir./wr. Joss Whedon
Guest cast: Max Perlich, Seth
Green, Kristine Sutherland,
Robia La Morte, James G.
MacDonald, James Marsters,
Juliet Landau, Armin
Shimerman

SEASON THREE – *main cast*
Sarah Michelle Gellar (Buffy
Summers). Nicholas Brendon
(Xander Harris). Alyson
Hannigan (Willow Rosenberg).
Charisma Carpenter (Cordelia
Chase). David Boreanaz
(Angel). Seth Green (Oz).
Anthony Stewart Head
(Rupert Giles).
©1998/1999.

29/9/1998 Anne
dir./wr. Joss Whedon
Guest cast: Kristine
Sutherland, Julia Lee, Carlos
Jacott, Mary-Pat Green, Chad
Todhunter
**6/10/1998 Dead Man's
Party**
dir. James Whitmore, Jr., wr.
Marti Noxon
Guest cast: Kristine
Sutherland, Nancy Lenehan,
Armin Shimerman

143

13/10/1998 Faith, Hope and Trick
dir. James A. Contner, wr. David Greenwalt
Guest cast: Kristine Sutherland, K. Todd Freeman, Fab Filippo, Jeremy Roberts, Eliza Dushku, Armin Shimerman

20/10/1998 Beauty and the Beasts
dir. James Whitmore, Jr., wr. Marti Noxon
Guest cast: Fab Filippo, John Patrick White, Danielle Weeks, Phill Lewis, Eliza Dushku

3/11/1998 Homecoming
dir./wr. David Greenwalt
Guest cast: K. Todd Freeman, Jeremy Ratchford, Fab Filippo, Ian Abercrombie, Harry Groener, Eliza Dushku

10/11/1998 Band Candy
dir. Michael Lange, wr. Jane Espenson
Guest cast: Kristine Sutherland, K. Todd Freeman, Robin Sachs, Harry Groener, Armin Shimerman

17/11/1998 Revelations
dir. James A. Contner, wr. Douglas Petrie
Guest cast: Serena Scott Thomas, Eliza Dushku

24/11/1998 Lover's Walk
dir. David Semel, wr. Dan Vebber
Guest cast: Kristine Sutherland, Harry Groener, James Marsters

8/12/1998 The Wish
dir. David Greenwalt, wr. Marti Noxon
Guest cast: Mark Metcalf, Emma Caulfield, Larry Bagby III, Mercedes McNab

15/12/1998 Amends
dir./wr. Joss Whedon
Guest cast: Kristine Sutherland, Saverio Guerra, Shane Barach, Edward Edwards, Cornelia Hayes O'Herlihy, Robia La Morte, Eliza Dushku

12/1/1999 Gingerbread
dir. James Whitmore, Jr., teleplay: Jane Espenson, story: Thania St. John, Jane Espenson
Guest cast: Kristine Sutherland, Elizabeth Anne Allen, Harry Groener, Jordan Baker, Armin Shimerman

19/1/1999 Helpless
dir. James A. Contner, wr. David Fury
Guest cast: Kristine Sutherland, Jeff Kober, Harris Yulin

26/1/1999 The Zeppo
dir. James Whitmore, Jr., wr. Dan Vebber
Guest cast: Saverio Guerra, Channon Roe, Michael Cudlitz, Eliza Dushku

9/2/1999 Bad Girls
dir. Michael Lange, wr. Douglas Petrie
Guest cast: Kristine Sutherland, Harry Groener, K. Todd Freeman, Jack Plotnick, Alexis Denisof, Christian Clemenson, Eliza Dushku

16/2/1999 Consequences
dir. Michael Gershman, wr. Marti Noxon
Guest cast: Kristine Sutherland, Harry Groener, K. Todd Freeman, Jack Plotnick, Alexis Denisof, James G. MacDonald, Eliza Dushku

23/2/1999 Doppelgangland
dir./wr. Joss Whedon
Guest cast: Harry Groener, Alexis Denisof, Emma Caulfield, Ethan Erickson, Eliza Dushku, Armin Shimerman

16/3/1999 Enemies
dir. David Grossman, wr. Douglas Petrie
Guest cast: Kristine Sutherland, Harry Groener, Alexis Denisof, Michael Manasser, Gary Bullock, Eliza Dushku

21/9/1999 Earshot
dir. Regis B. Kimble, wr. Jane Espenson

Guest cast: Kristine Sutherland, Alexis Denisof, Ethan Erickson, Danny Strong

4/5/1999 Choices
dir. James A. Contner, wr. David Fury
Guest cast: Kristine Sutherland, Harry Groener, Alexis Denisof, Eliza Dushku, Armin Shimerman

11/5/1999 The Prom
dir. David Solomon, wr. Marti Noxon
Guest cast: Kristine Sutherland, Alexis Denisof, Brad Kane, Emma Caulfield

18/5/1999 Graduation Day, part one
dir./wr. Joss Whedon
Guest cast: Kristine Sutherland, Harry Groener, Alexis Denisof, Mercedes McNab, Ethan Erickson, Emma Caulfield, Eliza Dushku, Armin Shimerman

13/7/1999 Graduation Day, part two
dir./wr. Joss Whedon
Guest cast: Harry Groener, Alexis Denisof, Danny Strong, Larry Bagby III, Mercedes McNab, Ethan Erickson, Eliza Dushku, Armin Shimerman

SEASON FOUR – *main cast*
Sarah Michelle Gellar (Buffy Summers). Nicholas Brendon (Xander Harris). Alyson Hannigan (Willow Rosenberg). Seth Green (Oz) [1–6]. James Marsters (Spike) [7–22]. Amber Benson (Tara Maclay). Anthony Stewart Head (Rupert Giles). ©1999/2000.

5/10/1999 The Freshman
dir./wr. Joss Whedon
Guest cast: Kristine Sutherland, Marc Blucas, Dagney Kerr, Pedro Balmaceda, Katharine Towne, Lindsay Crouse

12/10/1999 Living Conditions
dir. David Grossman, wr. Marti Noxon
Guest cast: Dagney Kerr, Adam Kaufman

19/10/1999 The Harsh Light of Day
dir. James A. Contner, wr. Jane Espenson
Guest cast: Emma Caulfield, Mercedes McNab, Adam Kaufman, James Marsters

26/10/1999 Fear Itself
dir. Tucker Gates, wr. David Fury
Guest cast: Kristine Sutherland, Marc Blucas, Emma Caulfield, Adam Kaufman, Lindsay Crouse

2/11/1999 Beer Bad
dir. David Solomon, wr. Tracey Forbes
Guest cast: Marc Blucas, Adam Kaufman, Paige Moss, Eric Matheny, Stephen M. Porter, Lindsay Crouse

9/11/1999 Wild at Heart
dir. David Grossman, wr. Marti Noxon
Guest cast: Marc Blucas, Paige Moss, James Marsters, Lindsay Crouse

16/11/1999 The Initiative
dir. James A. Contner, wr. Douglas Petrie
Guest cast: Marc Blucas, Mercedes McNab, Adam Kaufman, Bailey Chase, Leonard Roberts, Lindsay Crouse

23/11/1999 Pangs
dir. Michael Lange, wr. Jane Espenson
Guest cast: Marc Blucas, Mercedes McNab, Emma Caulfield, Leonard Roberts, Bailey Chase, Tod Thawley, David Boreanaz

30/11/1999 Something Blue
dir. Nick Marck, wr. Tracey Forbes
Guest cast: Marc Blucas, Emma Caulfield, Elizabeth Anne Allen

14/12/1999 Hush
dir./wr. Joss Whedon
Guest cast: Marc Blucas, Emma Caulfield, Leonard Roberts, Phina Oruche, Brooke Bloom, Jessica Townsend, Lindsay Crouse

18/1/2000 Doomed
dir. James A. Contner, wr. Marti Noxon, David Fury, Jane Espenson
Guest cast: Leonard Roberts, Bailey Chase, Ethan Erickson

25/1/2000 A New Man
dir. Michael Gershman, wr. Jane Espenson
Guest cast: Robin Sachs, Emma Caulfield, Lindsay Crouse

8/2/2000 The I in Team
dir. James A. Contner, wr. David Fury
Guest cast: George Hertzberg, Leonard Roberts, Bailey Chase, Jack Stehlin, Emma Caulfield, Lindsay Crouse

15/2/2000 Goodbye Iowa
dir. David Solomon, wr. Marti Noxon
Guest cast: George Hertzberg, Leonard Roberts, Bailey Chase, Jack Stehlin, J. B. Gaynor, Saverio Guerra, Emma Caulfield

22/2/2000 This Year's Girl
dir. Michael Gershman, wr. Douglas Petrie
Guest cast: Kristine Sutherland, Leonard Roberts, Bailey Chase, Chet Grissom, Alastair Duncan, Harry Groener, Eliza Dushku

29/2/2000 Who Are You?
dir./wr. Joss Whedon
Guest cast: Kristine Sutherland, Leonard Roberts, George Hertzberg, Chet Grissom, Alastair Duncan, Emma Caulfield, Eliza Dushku

4/4/2000 Superstar
dir. David Grossman, wr. Jane Espenson
Guest cast: Danny Strong,

Bailey Chase, Robert Patrick Benedict, John Saint Ryan, George Hertzberg, Emma Caulfield

25/4/2000 Where the Wild Things Are
dir. David Solomon, wr. Tracey Forbes
Guest cast: Leonard Roberts, Bailey Chase, Kathryn Joosten, Emma Caulfield

2/5/2000 New Moon Rising
dir. James A. Contner, wr. Marti Noxon
Guest cast: Leonard Roberts, Bailey Chase, Robert Patrick Benedict, Conor O'Farrell, George Hertzberg, Emma Caulfield, Seth Green

9/5/2000 The Yoko Factor
dir. David Grossman, wr. Doug Petrie
Guest cast: Leonard Roberts, Conor O'Farrell, George Hertzberg, Emma Caulfield, David Boreanaz

16/5/2000 Primeval
dir. James A. Contner, wr. David Fury
Guest cast: Leonard Roberts, Bailey Chase, Jack Stehlin, Conor O'Farrell, George Hertzberg, Emma Caulfield, Lindsay Crouse

23/5/2000 Restless
dir./wr. Joss Whedon
Guest cast: Kristine Sutherland, Mercedes McNab, David Wells, Michael Harney, George Hertzberg, Emma Caulfield, Seth Green, Armin Shimerman

SEASON FIVE – *main cast*
Sarah Michelle Gellar (Buffy Summers). Nicholas Brendon (Xander Harris). Alyson Hannigan (Willow Rosenberg). Marc Blucas (Riley) [1-10]. Emma Caulfield (Anya). Michelle Trachtenberg (Dawn Summers). James Marsters (Spike). Anthony Stewart Head (Rupert Giles). ©2000/2001.

145

26/9/2000 Buffy vs Dracula
dir. David Solomon, wr. Marti
Noxon
Guest cast: Rudolf Martin,
Michelle Trachtenberg, Amber
Benson, Kristine Sutherland
3/10/2000 Real Me
dir. David Grossman, wr.
David Fury
Guest cast: Mercedes McNab,
Bob Morrisey, Amber Benson,
Kristine Sutherland
10/10/2000 The
Replacement
dir. James A. Contner, wr.
Jane Espenson
Guest cast: Michael Bailey
Smith, Kristine Sutherland
17/10/2000 Out of My
Mind
dir. David Grossman, wr.
Rebecca Rand Kirshner
Guest cast: Mercedes McNab,
Bailey Chase, Charlie Weber,
Time Winters, Amber Benson,
Kristine Sutherland
24/10/2000 No Place Like
Home
dir. David Solomon, wr.
Douglas Petrie
Guest cast: Clare Kramer,
Charlie Weber, Ravil Isyanov,
Kristine Sutherland
7/11/2000 Family
dir./wr. Joss Whedon
Guest cast: Mercedes McNab,
Clare Kramer, Charlie Weber,
Amy Adams, Steve Rankin,
Amber Benson
14/11/2000 Fool for Love
dir. Nick Marck, wr. Douglas
Petrie
Guest cast: David Boreanaz,
Mercedes McNab, Julie Benz,
Juliet Landau, Kristine
Sutherland
21/11/2000 Shadow
dir. Daniel Attias, wr. David
Fury
Guest cast: Clare Kramer,
Charlie Weber, Kevin
Weisman, William Forward,
Amber Benson, Kristine
Sutherland

28/11/2000 Listening to Fear
dir. David Solomon, wr.
Rebecca Rand Kirshner
Guest cast: Charlie Weber,
Nick Chinlund, Kevin
Weisman, Randy Thompson,
Amber Benson, Kristine
Sutherland
19/12/2000 Into the
Woods
dir./wr. Marti Noxon
Guest cast: Bailey Chase,
Nick Chinlund, Kristine
Sutherland
9/1/2001 Triangle
dir. Christopher Hibler, wr.
Jane Espenson
Guest cast: Abraham Benrubi,
Amber Benson, Kristine
Sutherland
23/1/2001 Checkpoint
dir. Nick Marck, wr. Douglas
Petrie, Jane Espenson
Guest cast: Clare Kramer,
Charlie Weber, Cynthia
LaMontagne, Oliver
Muirhead, Kris Iyer, Kevin
Weisman, Troy T. Blendell,
Amber Benson, Harris Yulin,
Kristine Sutherland
6/2/2001 Blood Ties
dir. Michael Gershman, wr.
Steven S. DeKnight
Guest cast: Clare Kramer,
Charlie Weber, Troy T.
Blendell, Amber Benson,
Kristine Sutherland
13/2/2001 Crush
dir. Daniel Attias, wr. David
Fury
Guest cast: Mercedes McNab,
Charlie Weber, Amber
Benson, Juliet Landau,
Kristine Sutherland
20/2/2001 I Was Made to
Love You
dir. James A. Contner, wr.
Jane Espenson
Guest cast: Clare Kramer,
Charlie Weber, Shonda Farr,
Adam Busch, Troy T. Blendell,
Amber Benson, Kristine
Sutherland
27/2/2001 The Body
dir./wr. Joss Whedon

Guest cast: Randy Thompson,
Amber Benson, Kristine
Sutherland
17/4/2001 Forever
dir./wr. Marti Noxon
Guest cast: David Boreanaz,
Clare Kramer, Charlie Weber,
Troy T. Blendell, Amber
Benson, Joel Grey
24/4/2001 Intervention
dir. Michael Gershman, wr.
Jane Espenson
Guest cast: Clare Kramer,
Adam Busch, Troy T. Blendell,
Amber Benson
1/5/2001 Tough Love
dir. David Grossman, wr.
Rebecca Rand Kirshner
Guest cast: Clare Kramer,
Charlie Weber, Troy T.
Blendell, Anne Betancourt,
Leland Crooke, Amber Benson
8/5/2001 Spiral
dir. James A. Contner, wr.
Steven S. DeKnight
Guest cast: Clare Kramer,
Charlie Weber, Wade Andrew
Williams, Karim Prince,
Amber Benson
15/5/2001 The Weight of the
World
dir. David Solomon, wr.
Douglas Petrie
Guest cast: Clare Kramer,
Charlie Weber, Dean Butler,
Lily Knight, Bob Morrisey,
Amber Benson, Joel Grey,
Kristine Sutherland
22/5/2001 The Gift
dir./wr. Joss Whedon
Guest cast: Clare Kramer,
Charlie Weber, Amber
Benson, Joel Grey

SEASON SIX – *main cast*
Sarah Michelle Gellar (Buffy
Summers). Nicholas Brendon
(Xander Harris). Emma
Caulfield (Anya). Michelle
Trachtenberg (Dawn
Summers). James Marsters
(Spike). Alyson Hannigan
(Willow Rosenberg). Amber
Benson (Tara Maclay) [19]
©2001/2002.

146

2/10/2001 Bargaining, part one
dir. David Grossman, wr. Marti Noxon
Guest cast: Anthony Stewart Head, Franc Ross, Amber Benson
2/10/2001 Bargaining, part two
dir. David Grossman, wr. David Fury
Guest cast: Anthony Stewart Head, Franc Ross, Amber Benson
9/1/2001 After Life
dir. David Solomon, wr. Jane Espenson
Guest cast: Amber Benson
16/10/2001 Flooded
dir. Douglas Petrie, wr. Douglas Petrie, Jane Espenson
Guest cast: Anthony Stewart Head, Danny Strong, Adam Busch, Tom Lenk, Todd Stashwick, Amber Benson
23/10/2001 Life Serial
dir. Nick Marck, wr. David Fury, Jane Espenson
Guest cast: Anthony Stewart Head, Danny Strong, Adam Busch, Tom Lenk, Amber Benson
30/10/2001 All the Way
dir. David Solomon, wr. Steven S. DeKnight
Guest cast: Anthony Stewart Head, John O'Leary, Kavan Reece, Amber Tamblyn, Dave Power, Amber Benson
6/11/2001 Once More, with Feeling
dir./wr. Joss Whedon
Guest cast: Anthony Stewart Head, Hinton Battle, Amber Benson
13/11/2001 Tabula Rasa
dir. David Grossman, wr. Rebecca Rand Kirshner
Guest cast: Anthony Stewart Head, Amber Benson
20/11/2001 Smashed
dir. Turi Meyer, wr. Drew Z. Greenberg

Guest cast: Danny Strong, Adam Busch, Tom Lenk, Elizabeth Anne Allen, Amber Benson
27/11/2001 Wrecked
dir. David Solomon, wr. Marti Noxon
Guest cast: Elizabeth Anne Allen, Jeff Kober, Amber Benson
8/1/2002 Gone
dir./wr. David Fury
Guest cast: Danny Strong, Adam Busch, Tom Lenk, Daniel Hagen, Susan Ruttan
29/1/2002 Doublemeat Palace
dir. Nick Marck, wr. Jane Espenson
Guest cast: Elizabeth Anne Allen, Pat Crawford Brown, Brent Hinkley, Kirsten Nelson, Kali Rocha
5/2/2002 Dead Things
dir. James A. Contner, wr. Steven S. DeKnight
Guest cast: Danny Strong, Adam Busch, Tom Lenk, Amelinda Embry, Amber Benson
12/2/2002 Older and Far Away
dir. Michael Gershman, wr. Drew Z. Greenberg
Guest cast: Kali Rocha, Ryan Browning, Amber Benson
26/2/2002 As You Were
dir./wr. Douglas Petrie
Guest cast: Marc Blucas, Ivana Milicevic
5/3/2002 Hell's Bells
dir. David Solomon, wr. Rebecca Rand Kirshner
Guest cast: Casey Sander, Kali Rocha, Andy Umberger, Lee Garlington, Jan Hoag, George D. Wallace, Amber Benson, Steven Gilborn
12/3/2002 Normal Again
dir. Rick Rosenthal, wr. Diego Gutierrez
Guest cast: Danny Strong, Adam Busch, Tom Lenk, Dean Butler, Michael Warren, Kirsten Nelson, Amber Benson, Kristine Sutherland

30/4/2002 Entropy
dir. James A. Contner, wr. Drew Z. Greenberg
Guest cast: Danny Strong, Adam Busch, Tom Lenk, Kali Rocha, Amber Benson
7/5/2002 Seeing Red
dir. Michael Gershman, wr. Steven S. DeKnight
Guest cast: Danny Strong, Adam Busch, Tom Lenk, Amy Hathaway, Nichole Hiltz
14/5/2002 Villains
dir. David Solomon, wr. Marti Noxon
Guest cast: Danny Strong, Adam Busch, Tom Lenk, Jeff Kober, Amelinda Embry, Amber Benson
21/5/2002 Two to Go
dir. Bill Norton, wr. Douglas Petrie
Guest cast: Danny Strong, Tom Lenk, Jeff Kober
21/5/2002 Grave
dir. James A. Contner, wr. David Fury
Guest cast: Anthony Stewart Head, Danny Strong, Tom Lenk

SEASON SEVEN – *main cast*
Sarah Michelle Gellar (Buffy Summers). Nicholas Brendon (Xander Harris). Emma Caulfield (Anya). Michelle Trachtenberg (Dawn Summers). James Marsters (Spike). Alyson Hannigan (Willow Rosenberg). ©2002/2003. Twentieth Century Fox Film Corporation

24/9/2002 Lessons
dir. David Solomon, wr. Joss Whedon
Guest cast: Anthony Stewart Head, Kali Rocha, D. B. Woodside
1/10/2002 Beneath You
dir. Nick Marck, wr. Douglas Petrie
Guest cast: Anthony Stewart Head, Kaarina Aufranc, D. B. Woodside

147

8/10/2002 Same Time, Same Place
dir. James A. Contner, wr. Jane Espenson
Guest cast: none
15/10/2002 Help
dir. Rick Rosenthal, wr. Rebecca Rand Kirshner
Guest cast: Azura Skye, Zachary Bryan, Glenn Morshower, Rick Gonzalez, Kevin Christy, Sarah Hagan, Beth Skipp, Anthony Harrell, Jarrett Lennon, D. B. Woodside
22/10/2002 Selfless
dir. David Solomon, wr. Drew Goddard
Guest cast: Abraham Benrubi, Andy Umberger, Kali Rocha, Joyce Guy, Jennifer Shon
5/11/2002 Him
dir. Michael Gershman, wr. Drew Z. Greenberg
Guest cast: Thad Luckinbill, Brandon Keener, D. B. Woodside
12/11/2002 Conversations with Dead People
dir. Nick Marck, wr. Jane Espenson, Drew Goddard
Guest cast: Danny Strong, Adam Busch, Tom Lenk, Jonathan M. Woodward, Azura Skye, Kristine Sutherland
19/11/2002 Sleeper
dir. Alan J. Levi, wr. David Fury, Jane Espenson
Guest cast: Anthony Stewart Head, Robinne Lee, Rob Nagle
26/11/2002 Never Leave Me
dir. David Solomon, wr. Drew Goddard
Guest cast: Danny Strong, Adam Busch, Tom Lenk, Cynthia LaMontagne, Oliver Muirhead, Kris Iyer, Harris Yulin, D. B. Woodside

17/12/2002 Bring on the Night
dir. David Grossman, wr. Marti Noxon, Douglas Petrie
Guest cast: Anthony Stewart Head, Kristine Sutherland, Tom Lenk, Iyari Limon, Clara Bryant, Courtnee Draper, Juliet Landau, D. B. Woodside
7/1/2003 Showtime
dir. Michael Grossman, wr. David Fury
Guest cast: Anthony Stewart Head, Tom Lenk, Iyari Limon, Clara Bryant, Indigo, Amanda Fuller
21/1/2003 Potential
dir. James A. Contner, wr. Rebecca Rand Kirshner
Guest cast: Tom Lenk, Iyari Limon, Clara Bryant, Indigo
4/2/2003 The Killer in Me
dir. David Solomon, wr. Drew Z. Greenberg
Guest cast: Anthony Stewart Head, Adam Busch, Tom Lenk, Iyari Limon, Elizabeth Anne Allen, Megalyn Echikunwoke, Rif Huton
11/2/2003 First Date
dir. David Grossman, wr. Jane Espenson
Guest cast: Anthony Stewart Head, Ashanti, Danny Strong, Tom Lenk, Iyari Limon, Sarah Hagan, Kristy Wu, K. D. Aubert, D. B. Woodside
18/2/2003 Get It Done
dir./wr. Douglas Petrie
Guest cast: Tom Lenk, Iyari Limon, Clara Bryant, Sarah Hagan, Indigo, Kristy Wu, Lalaine, D. B. Woodside
25/2/2003 Storyteller
dir. Marita Grabiak, wr. Jane Espenson
Guest cast: Danny Strong, Adam Busch, Tom Lenk, Iyari Limon, Sarah Hagan, Indigo, D. B. Woodside

25/3/2003 Lies My Parents Told Me
dir. David Fury, wr. David Fury, Drew Goddard
Guest cast: Anthony Stewart Head, Tom Lenk, Iyari Limon, Indigo, Caroline Lagerfelt, K. D. Aubert, Juliet Landau, D. B. Woodside
15/4/2003 Dirty Girls
dir. Michael Gershman, wr. Drew Goddard
Guest cast: Anthony Stewart Head, Eliza Dushku, Nathan Fillion, Tom Lenk, Iyari Limon, Indigo, Clara Bryant, Sarah Hagan, Kristy Wu, D. B. Woodside
29/4/2003 Empty Places
dir. James A. Contner, wr. Drew Z. Greenberg
Guest cast: Anthony Stewart Head, Eliza Dushku, Nathan Fillion, Tom Lenk, Iyari Limon, Indigo, Sarah Hagan, Kristy Wu, Dorian Missic, Larry Clarke, D. B. Woodside
6/5/2003 Touched
dir. David Solomon, wr. Rebecca Rand Kirshner
Guest cast: Anthony Stewart Head, Eliza Dushku, Nathan Fillion, Tom Lenk, Iyari Limon, Sarah Hagan, Harry Groener, D. B. Woodside
13/5/2003 End of Days
dir. Marita Grabiak, wr. Douglas Petrie, Jane Espenson
Guest cast: Anthony Stewart Head, Eliza Dushku, Nathan Fillion, David Boreanaz, Tom Lenk, Iyari Limon, Sarah Hagan, Christine Healy
20/5/2003 Chosen
dir./wr. Joss Whedon
Guest cast: Anthony Stewart Head, Eliza Dushku, Nathan Fillion, David Boreanaz, Tom Lenk, Iyari Limon, Sarah Hagan, Indigo, D. B. Woodside

Sources

Books and Articles

Adams, Michael, *Slayer Slang: A* Buffy the Vampire Slayer *Lexicon* (New York: Oxford University Press, 2003).

Clover, Carol J., *Men, Women and Chainsaws: Gender in the Modern Horror Film* (London: BFI, 1992).

Cusick, Richie Tankersley (based on the screenplay by Joss Whedon), *Buffy the Vampire Slayer* (New York: Pocket Books, 1992).

Fassbender, Tom and Jim Pascoe, *The Death of Buffy* (Milwaukie, OR: Dark Horse Comics, 2002).

——, *False Memories* (Milwaukie, OR: Dark Horse Comics, 2002).

Golden, Christopher and Nancy Holder, Buffy the Vampire Slayer: *The Watcher's Guide* (New York: Pocket Books, 1998).

Golden, Christopher and Daniel Brereton, Buffy the Vampire Slayer: *The Origin* (Milwaukie, OR: Dark Horse Comics, 1999).

Holder, Nancy with Jeff Mariotte and Maryelizabeth Hart, Buffy the Vampire Slayer: *The Watcher's Guide Volume 2* (New York: Pocket Books, 2000).

Lewis, Jon E. and Penny Stempel, *Cult TV* (London: Pavilion, 1996).

Lobdell, Scott and Fabian Nicieza, *Viva Las Buffy* (Milwaukie, OR: Dark Horse Comics, 2003).

Melton, J. Gordon, *The Vampire Book* (Detroit, MI: Visible Ink Press, 1994).

Pirie, David, *The Vampire Cinema* (Feltham, Middlesex: Hamlyn, 1977).

Ruditis, Paul, Buffy the Vampire Slayer: *The Watcher's Guide Volume 3* (New York: Pocket Books, 2004).

Weiss, Andrea, *Vampires and Violets: Lesbians in Film* (New York: Penguin, 1993).

Whedon, Joss, *Fray* (Milwaukie, OR: Dark Horse Comics, 2003).

—— *Astonishing X-Men* (New York: Marvel Comics, 2004).

—— et al., *Tales of the Slayers* (Milwaukie, OR: Dark Horse Comics, 2001).

—— et al., *Tales of the Vampires* (Milwaukie, OR: Dark Horse Comics, 2004).

Websites

The Buffy Body Count <homepage.mac.com/dsample>

The Buffy/Giles Fanfiction Archive <www.buffygiles.com/archive>

The Buffy Trivia Guide <www.restlessbtvs.com/trivia>

The Classic TV Database <www.classic-tv.com>

CulTV <users.metronet.co.uk/cultv>

Fametracker: The Farmer's Almanac of Celebrity Worth <www.fametracker.com> (alas, the Fametracker Forums, which provided me with many hours of rib-tickling pleasure, have now been dismantled)

Intensities: the Journal of Cult Media <www.cult-media.com/issue1/Ahill.htm>

The Internet Movie Database <www.imdb.com>

Jump the Shark: Chronicling the Moments When TV Shows Go Downhill <www.jumptheshark.com>

Memorable TV <www.memorabletv.com>

The Onion A.V. Club <www.theonionavclub.com>

Scifilm <www.scifilm.org>

Sitcoms Online <www.sitcomsonline.com>

The Slayer.Net <www.theslayer.net>

Television without Pity <www.televisionwithoutpity.com>

TV Tome: Guide to the Television Shows You Love (Down with TV.com! Bring back TV Tome!)

Variety.com <www.variety.com/index.asp>

Index

Page numbers in *italics* indicate illustrations.

153